SUCCESSFULLY SEEKING GOD . . .

HOW TO TAP into the WISDOM OF GOD

BASED ON THE WISDOM AND METHODS OF DANIEL

William D. Banks

How To Tap Into The Wisdom of God,
By William D. Banks
ISBN # 089228-121-9

Impact Christian Books, Inc.
332 Leffingwell Ave., Suite 101,
Kirkwood, MO 63122

Cover Design: Susan Blake

Printed in the United States of America

ACKNOWLEDGMENTS

I want to express my indebtedness to my wonderful wife of thirty-five years, Sue, who has kept the house functioning, and who, along with my sons sacrificed time with me, during this writing project.

Appreciation is also due to Pam Miltenberger for her assistance with proofing and grammar on many of my books including this one, and to Sue Blake, my talented cover artist.

I am also indebted to the faithful and patient "little flock" of the Thursday Night Meetings who have borne with me for twenty-five years and drawn the best out of me, as I have taught much of this material in embryonic form.

DEDICATION

I dedicate this labor of love to the Father, Son, and Holy Spirit all of Whom are vitally involved in the process of revealing and communicating truth to God's people.

With reverence and awe I humbly offer this book in the hope that it will serve to stimulate hunger and thirst among His people, and those who may be caused to seek the Author of all wisdom and knowledge.

Other Books by this Author:

Alive Again!	1977
Ministering to Abortion's Aftermath	1982
The Heavens Declare...	1985
Power for Deliverance:	
Songs of Deliverance	1987
Deliverance From Fat	1988
Deliverance for Children and Teens	1989
Deliverance From Childlessness	1990
Three Kinds of Faith for Healing	1992
Everything Is Possible	1995

by Sue Banks

The Little Skunk,
Childrens' Introduction to Deliverance 1995

CONTENTS

AUTHOR'S PREFACE

Fresh revelation from God may not be the fountain of youth, but it is the fountain of life. I have never felt more alive, more invigorated, more joyful, more in tune with God than when I have received enlightenment by His Spirit, and was shown fresh, exciting truths in His word. "Exciting" is an appropriately descriptive word, for there is a tremendous excitement within my spirit and my soul when God reveals something to me. Divine energy courses through my body much as if I'd touched a live wire.

The very word "enthusiasm" comes from two Greek root words *en-theo,* God within. The world may observe our joyful enthusiasm but little imagine that its source is God. In fact, it is symptomatic of a kingdom which they cannot even see, which *is not meat and drink; but righteousness, and peace, and joy in the Holy Ghost.* Rom. 14:17

While verifying that definition, I was delightfully surprised to discover that the first definition of enthusiasm according to Webster was "belief in special revelations of the Holy Spirit." Now, I am even more enthusiastic, for I definitely believe in the present role of the Holy Spirit as the **revealer of God's truths.**

The promises and the blessing to be discussed are for believers only. Are you eligible? Have you been born again as a child into the Kingdom of God? Are you properly related to the Holy Spirit, the Teacher and Revealer of God's secrets?

There is a good bit of Scripture included in this book, and the reason is fairly simple. As the Holy Spirit is invited and allowed to explain the Scripture, He will quicken truths to us. He frequently allows us to see things in the Word that we have never previously perceived. In addition, we simply allow Scripture to explain Scripture, which allows us to move beyond the mere opinions of man.

Receiving such fresh revelation is an additional confirmation of His love for you, a confirmation of your status as His child and His friend; friends share things with one another, especially secrets. **You do have a Friend, God Himself, who wishes to share some of His secrets with you.**

What Mordecai said to Esther, *who knoweth whether thou art come to the kingdom for such a time as this?* Esther 4:14 may be applicable to this author as well. Perhaps it was for just this purpose that the Lord Jesus Christ spared my life from terminal cancer twenty-five years ago, so I could discover and share the truths of **how to receive His wisdom**. For the past twenty-five years I have been conscientiously seeking Him and desiring to learn how to hear, learn, from Him. During those years many people have asked the question, "How can I hear from God?" Usually also complaining, God never speaks to them or that they have never heard God speak.

I can identify with the desires of those individuals. Every one of us wants to hear from God; every one of us feels the need from time to time of a personal word, or encouragement from God. I can identify with those who have never heard God speak audibly to them, for I have not. I confess to envying several minister friends who heard an audible call into the ministry. I did not.

Apparently there are a great many of us whom God has chosen to guide via circumstances and in ways other than an audible voice. For example, I was led into the ministry of healing and deliverance by my own need for healing, when He healed me of terminal cancer. Afterwards I desired to share both the blessing of healing which I had received, and what I had discovered in the Word of God regarding the availability of God's healing power. I found that when I stepped out in faith and prayed for others, God met me and blessed by healing most of those for whom we prayed.

In recent years I realized that *I have been learning from God*; I have been receiving revelations from Him by the Holy Spirit for twenty-five years. I did not fully realize it, but on numerous occasions after sharing revelations concerning passages of Scripture, minister friends I greatly respected and considered my elders in the faith, made comments such as, "What commentary did you find that in? That interpretation is right on, and it's tremendous." When people asked where I went to seminary, I usually joked and said I attended "the School of the Spirit," until one young brother in all seriousness asked me for the school's address.

I have come to realize there are certain principles and keys I have learned that aid me in learning from God, and that allow me to tap into the wisdom of God. The keys to unlocking the secrets of the wisdom of the universe are in these pages. Among them is the key to immortal life, and perhaps even the key to the fountain of youth.

Jesus Christ is the Wisdom of God as Paul declared in I Corinthians 1:24b, *Christ the power of God, and the wisdom of God.*

The Privilege of Fellowship With God

One great privilege believers have which is often taken for granted, or greatly underestimated, is fellowship with God. What a truly awesome thought that the great Creator God of the Universe is willing to meet with human beings. If you were told you would have an opportunity to meet the

Queen of England, the President of the United States or perhaps Billy Graham, you would be excited and looking forward to that day with great anticipation. However, there is One far greater than any of these personages who is willing to meet with you, and has, in fact, invited you to meet with Him, to have intimate fellowship with Him. Regrettably, most of us have taken both Him and His invitation lightly.

We readily criticize the men in the parable of the great supper who asked to be excused from attending God's banquet because of their worldly interests. Yet, how often do we, like them, make light of His invitation and make excuses for not spending time in prayer and fellowship with God? One of the greatest privileges in the universe should be to have an audience with, and to spend time with, the Owner and Ruler of the Universe.

What greater honor or privilege could there be, than for one to have fellowship with God, and beyond that to have the Creator of the Universe share a secret with you or to allow *you* to tap into *His* wisdom?

William D. Banks
Kirkwood, Missouri
July 4, 1996

[I, (Paul)]...*do not cease to pray for you, and to desire that ye might be filled with the knowledge of his will in all wisdom and spiritual understanding; That ye might walk worthy of the Lord unto all pleasing, being fruitful in every good work, and increasing in the knowledge of God.*

Col. 1:10

CHAPTER ONE

GOD WANTS TO GIVE WISDOM

When ye therefore shall see the abomination of desolation, spoken of by Daniel the prophet, stand in the holy place, (whoso readeth, let him understand:) Mat. 24:15

In His quote from the Book of Daniel, the Lord Jesus Christ, Himself, admonishes us to apply ourselves prayerfully to understand the words of Daniel, because, His meaning is clear, they will have significance for us today.

Although I do not pretend to be an expert on the subject of hearing from God, I do believe that God has blessed me with some very simple keys and principles that are helpful to anyone willing to diligently employ them to discover for themselves ***How To Tap Into The Wisdom of God.*** The Book of Daniel contains clues to obtaining secrets and truth from God, but first there is something we must know.

To receive truth from God we must find promises in the Word, and come to fully believe that it is indeed God's will to reveal truth to us. Faith is crucial and can only exist as we know it to be God's will to give us His truth, His secrets, His knowledge, and His wisdom.

Faith Is Crucial to Understanding the Things of God

In order that we might have our faith built to receive wisdom from God, there is a question that we must have answered: Does God want to reveal His truth to His people, and more specifically, *to me*?

There is a basic truth concerning the establishing of faith to receive from God which was revealed to me more than twenty-five years ago. As a terminal cancer patient, I was seeking God's will regarding healing. For my faith to exist it was essential to know what His will was regarding what I was seeking.

We, of course, know that God is Omniscient; He sees and knows all things. There is no question that He possesses the ability to tell us anything we may need to know (His ability is not in question), but the point that is in question is whether it is His will, His desire, His intent, to do so, to me as an individual.

While seeking His truth about healing, it was obvious that He possessed the power to heal me; my question: was if it was *His will*, desire, intent to heal me.[1]

To know that someone has the ability to do something is not sufficient to create faith that he will do it. Thus there is a missing ingredient that must be added to our knowledge of a person's ability to do the thing needed: we must also know that it is *the will*, the desire, the intent of that person to do the thing that we are requesting.

At the time I was seeking healing, the Lord quickened

[1] The Scriptural answers which He gave to answer my specific questions regarding healing are related in a chapter entitled, "Is It God's Will to Heal You?" in my book *Alive Again!*

His truth to me in a formula-like statement: "It is impossible to have faith in God to do anything that we do not know to be the will of God." It may be easier to grasp this truth if it is stated negatively: "It is impossible to have faith in God to do anything that we think God doesn't want to do!"

Let that truth sink in. Reread it; let God burn that into your heart, because it is a key to truth, and to victory in Him! We must know that it **is God's will to give us His wisdom**.

Because the Word of God tells us in Hebrews *that God is no respecter of persons,* we can assume that if He has promised, or given, wisdom to any believer, or to any of His children, then it should be available to all believers. Such promises are predicated upon the supposition that one is a believer, properly related to Him as His child by the new birth.

Faith to Receive Will "Come"

If a believer has not heard the truth about something available to him in God, he cannot have any faith to receive it. His faith is dead! The person who is hopeless has given up on faith, or has never known it. Hope is a basis for faith; faith is the evidence of hope. Faith or expectation comes from the study of the Word of God, finding His promises applicable to you and your situation, and fellowship with the Holy Spirit.

Hope is the prelude to faith, and leads us to assurance, full confidence, trust in Him to perform the thing needed, which is faith.

When faith is present, the answer is imminent. Faith is like a conduit for God's energy. When we have hope that

God will reveal His truth to us, the faith to receive will come. Therefore, if we are seeking God's help or His divine will in a given situation, we must have His revelation; faith allows us to receive and act upon His word to us.

Through faith we understand. Heb. 11:3a

Faith has to precede receiving and understanding: We must believe and then we will understand.

I had fainted, unless I had believed to see. Psa. 27:13a

We must believe, have faith, first in order to be able to see (or hear). Or, as Jesus stated the principle even more clearly to Martha:

Said I not unto thee, that, if thou wouldest believe, thou shouldest see? John 11:40

Notice that Jesus clearly predicates seeing, upon first believing. This is a Biblical truth regardless of how much, like Thomas, we'd prefer to have it the other way.

But he said unto them, Except I shall see in his hands the print of the nails, and put my finger into the print of the nails, and thrust my hand into his side, I will not believe. John 20:25

Jesus established this principle, of believing preceding seeing, again to Nicodemus,

Except a man be born again, he cannot see the kingdom of God. John 3:3b

It is evident that we must *believe we shall receive* before we are eligible to receive, therefore a question must be answered. *Dare we hope that it is God's will for us to receive His wisdom?*

God Does Want Man to Know!

And the Lord said, Shall I hide from Abraham that thing which I do; Gen. 18:17

Surely the Lord God will do nothing, but he revealeth his secret unto his servants the prophets. Amos 3:7

And said, If thou wilt diligently hearken to the voice of the Lord thy God. Exo. 15:26

"Diligently hearken" in the Hebrew is "if listening thou wilt listen." How can we know for sure that God wants to reveal His truth, especially His as-yet-hidden truths to His children? We can only know this on the basis of His Word, and especially on the basis of any promises which we find in His Word. **God and his truth always meet us on the basis of a promise in His Word.** We cannot have faith to expect to receive unless we have a promise or a scriptural precedent, i.e., there is more to the Word of God than mere words and printers' ink on paper. Jesus stated that fact in John 6:63 when He said His words *are Spirit, and they are Life!*

But ye, brethren, are not in darkness. 1 Thes. 5:4

Ye are a chosen generation...of him who hath called you out of darkness into his marvellous light. 1 Pet. 2:9

Keep in mind that God especially wants you to know all the facts about Jesus; His pre-existence; His birth (humanity); and His resurrection (His divinity); to know His will and word, which, of course, since He and the Father are One, will also be the will and word of the Father! It is true that *The secret things belong unto the Lord.* (Deut. 29:29a), but God clearly wills to reveal truth to us. Jesus came that we might hear new truth that would set us free.

The Godhead itself is the most reliable witness to answer our question, but other proofs have also been given by God. He has gone to great lengths to verify that His will is to reveal not just His secrets to us, but all things and all truth!

Eight Proofs God Reveals His Will to Man

1 The Father's Ministry

God the Father sent prophets, such as Daniel, to reveal His ways, will, and Word, often at great risk to their lives. Why would God knowingly risk a believer's life if the mission were not His will and very important to Him.

Hearken to the words of my servants the prophets, whom I sent unto you, both rising up early, and sending them

Jer. 26:5

The commissioning of messengers to reveal His will, is illustrated by Jesus in the parable of His Father's vineyard in Matthew 21:34-37.

And...he sent his servants...Again, he sent other servants more than the first...last of all he sent unto them his son, saying, They will reverence my son.

2 **Jesus' Ministry**: He gave truth in parables.

Jesus' role as Prophet was accomplished through the parables He told as prophesied in the Old Testament.

All these things spake Jesus unto the multitude in parables; and without a parable spake he not unto them: "That it might be fulfilled which was spoken by the prophet, saying, I will open my mouth in parables; I ***will utter things which have been kept secret*** *from the foundation of the world."*

Mat. 13:34-35

Jesus is Himself *the Truth*, and He also gave us the Father's Truth.

Jesus saith...I am the way, the truth, and the life.

John 14:6a

Ye sent unto John, and he bare witness unto the truth.

John 5:33

For I have given unto them the words which thou gavest me...I have given them thy word. John 17:8a,14a

It remains the will of Jesus to cause men to understand the riches and hidden mysteries of God's Word, even after His resurrection, because He gave understanding to two men journeying to Emmaus.

Then opened he their understanding, that they might understand the scriptures. Luke 24:45

3 Holy Spirit's Ministry

Jesus promised that after His departure the Holy Spirit would continue ministering His truth. He has been sent *to reveal* (future tense) all things and all truth to the faithful.

But the Comforter, which is the Holy Ghost, whom the Father will send in my name, he ***shall teach*** *you* ***all things****, and bring* ***all things*** *to your remembrance, whatsoever I have said unto you.* John 14:26

Howbeit when he, the ***Spirit of truth****, is come, he* ***will guide*** *you into* ***all truth****: for he shall not speak of himself; but whatsoever he shall hear, that shall he speak:* ***and he will show you things to come.*** John 16:13

One of the chief ministries of the Holy Spirit is to reveal to us the things that Jesus has said: to make His truth meaningful and relevant to us for our lives.

He answered and said unto them, Because it is given unto you to know the mysteries of the kingdom of heaven, but to them it is not given. For whosoever hath, to him shall be given, and he shall have more abundance: but whosoever hath not, from him shall be taken away even that he hath. Therefore speak I to them in parables: because they seeing see not; and hearing they hear not, neither do they understand. Mat. 13:11-13

4 The Gifts of the Spirit

Six of the nine gifts of the Spirit have to do with God offering supernatural communication with man: God somehow imparting, communicating or conveying truth or knowledge to us. All of the following gifts listed in bold type relate to a supernatural impartation of knowledge or truth.

Now concerning spiritual gifts, brethren, I would not have you ignorant. For to one is given by the Spirit the ***word of wisdom****; to another the* ***word of knowledge*** *by the same Spirit; To another faith by the same Spirit; to another the gifts of healing by the same Spirit; To another the working of miracles; to another* ***prophecy****; to another* ***discerning of spirits****; to another* ***divers kinds of tongues****; to another the* ***interpretation of tongues.*** 1 Cor. 12:1,8-10

5 Fivefold Ministry Gift of Gifted Men

And he gave some, apostles; and some, prophets; and some, evangelists; and some, pastors and teachers; For the perfecting of the saints, for the work of the ministry, for the edifying of the body of Christ. Eph. 4:11-12

Each of these gifted individuals, the apostles, prophets, evangelists, teachers and pastors, has a role to play in communicating God's words, wisdom, and truth to his people, with the express goal of building them up.

6 Supernatural Confirmation of His Truth

Further, it is very clear that He wants us to know truth, because He has said He would confirm His truth to us with signs and wonders following, wonders which attest to His truth. Inherent in a need to confirm His Word miraculously is the assumption that His truth will be difficult for us to accept or believe, (i.e. "You shall not die." "Shall live forever in heaven.")

Behold, ye despisers, and wonder, and perish: for I work a work in your days, a work which ye shall in no wise believe, though a man declare it unto you. Acts 13:41

Thus, He not only will give us truth, but will also confirm it to us as truth with supernatural accompaniments.

And they went forth...the Lord working with them, and confirming the word with signs following. Mark 16:20

7 The Word of God

Sanctify them through thy truth: thy word is truth.
John 17:17

The Word of God is itself truth; it is a manifest expression of God's will to instruct man, and contains repeated indications and promises of God's continuing will to reveal Himself and His secrets to the people whom He has chosen. Secrets, by definition, are intended to be shared by friends and revealed at the proper time.

The written Word of God itself is intended to communicate His truth to us, new depths of truth and meaning in His word. I love the Word of God. After prospecting for precious stones in my youth, I see many similarities between the precious Word of God and the most precious of gems, the diamond

The Word is like a diamond. I may catch a glimpse of a facet of truth that appears blue. But as light is brought to bear upon it from a different vantage point, it offers to someone else a flash of truth that is yellow. Upon looking at my own truth later, it may seem to be violet, or perhaps I may even be able to see some of the yellow that was seen by my brother. The Word hasn't changed but I have changed. Each time we approach the Word of God we have a slightly different perspective. We have changed; actually we have *been changed*, and hopefully are being matured by our experiences. Reading the same passage later after a new set of experiences, we are able to see new depths of truth in it because our understanding has grown through our experiences.

Another indication that God intends for all His children to be recipients of His revelations is contained in the following verse:

*When ye come together, **every one of you** hath a psalm, hath a doctrine, **hath a revelation**, hath a tongue, hath an interpretation* [2] 1 Cor. 14:26

It is evident, from this passage that when the church body assembles, God expects (intends) that everyone (every member of the body present) be able to bring forth a song, a teaching, a revelation, a tongue or an interpretation.

8 A Final Proof

Jesus Himself promised that contained within His parables are things which have been kept secret from the foundation of the world. In John He promised the ministry of the Holy Spirit would include continuing revelation of truth to believers after He Himself had gone away.

*But the Comforter, which is the Holy Ghost, whom the Father will send in my name, he shall **teach you all things**,*

[2] You may have noticed that I have corrected the sequence of the last three listed occurrences. The Greek text correctly places "the interpretation" directly after "the tongue" in this passage just as it occurs in practice.

and bring ***all things to your remembrance****, whatsoever I have said unto you.* John 14:26

Howbeit when he, the Spirit of truth, is come, he will guide you ***into all truth****: for he shall not speak of himself; but whatsoever he shall hear, that shall he speak: and* ***he will show you things to come****. He shall glorify me: for* ***he shall*** *receive of mine, and* ***shall show it unto you****.* John 16:13-14

It is exciting that Jesus not only promises the Holy Spirit shall teach us all things, and shall bring all things to our remembrance, but also that He will show us things to come. He states that the Holy Spirit shall receive and shall show. "Shall" indicates future action; thus Jesus is making it clear that there are things to be revealed in the future after His ascension, by the Holy Spirit. This is contrary to our theological traditions which would have us believe that God somehow became mute after the Holy Scriptures were completed. Jesus Himself stated it plainly:

I have yet many things to say unto you, but ye cannot bear them now. John 16:12

Jesus emphasized this same truth a verse earlier in John when He specifically stated that there were truths that He wished to communicate, but that His hearers were not yet ready. So it is with many of us; we aren't yet ready to hear things He had to tell us in the past. Hopefully I am more open to hear His truth today than I was twenty-five years ago, and I pray that I will be still more open to what He will tell me tomorrow, or next year than I am today.

Thus, Jesus has commissioned us to hear, and the Holy Spirit to teach us, the new things that He will choose to have revealed. Anything God does not choose to reveal, He will not reveal, but the things that He has chosen to reveal are revealed to us, with the goal that we might be able to walk in obedience to Him and His will, as expressed in His Word. He commissions us to receive His truth which the Scriptures call "hidden things" and He commissions the Holy Spirit to teach us *all things* and to *show* us *things to come.* It is obvious that God will not reveal anything He does not wish to reveal. But He desires, loves, and longs to reveal Himself, His Son, His Spirit, and His word to His people.

Surely the Lord God will do nothing, but he revealeth his secret unto his servants the prophets. Amos 3:7

Through Amos He reveals that everything He does will be revealed as His secret to be shared with His servants. A secret is meant to be shared between friends. God does not have to reveal His secrets, but He chooses to do so, and receives glory and creates faith by revealing future events before they occur, as Jesus makes clear:

And now I have told you before it come to pass, that, when it is come to pass, ye might believe. John 14:29

Remember...for I am God, and there is none else; I am God, and there is none like me, Declaring the end from the beginning, and from ancient times the things that are not yet done, saying,..I have spoken it, I will also bring it to pass; I have purposed it, I will also do it. Isa. 46:9,10,11

Thus, it is clear that God desires to give wisdom to His children. Our question now is How to gain entry to God's storehouse of wisdom.

Scriptures Introducing Chapter Two

One thing have I desired of the Lord, that will I seek after; that I may dwell in the house of the Lord all the days of my life, to behold the beauty of the Lord, and to inquire in his temple. Psa. 27:4

My heart said unto thee, Thy face, Lord, will I seek. Psa. 27:8

Teach me thy way, O Lord, and lead me in a plain path, because of mine enemies. Psa. 27:11

Wait on the Lord: be of good courage, and he shall strengthen thine heart: wait, I say, on the Lord. Psa. 27:14

*The Lord God hath given me the tongue of the learned, that I should know how to speak a word in season to him that is weary: he wakeneth morning by morning, he wakeneth mine ear to hear as the learned.** Isa. 50:4

* "Learned" is rendered "disciple" in some translations.

CHAPTER TWO

THE DOOR OF ENTRY TO GOD'S TREASURE HOUSE OF WISDOM

We can regard the Word of God as the door to a vast storehouse of knowledge. Recall that Jesus, the *Logos*, the Word of God, referred to Himself as the Door in John 10:9. Exterior doors present an obstacle to entering. Such doors serve a dual purpose: on the one hand they prevent the uninvited from gaining access to the valuables within the house; on the other, they permit friends and family to enter.

The Owner has the keys which unlock the door. Like the door to your own heart, this door is latched from within. Once you have gained entry to the house, you will see that even a child can easily open the door from within, because doors are readily opened by those inside, or by those to whom the Owner has entrusted the keys. Similarly, once a truth is revealed to us, we are amazed that we had not seen it previously.

Our approach to the Word of God is strongly influenced by our attitude toward the Author. If we are sure that the Author is God, then we will expect His book to contain more than mere human concepts. He is supernatural, therefore His book will be a miracle-book. If someone gave you an ordinary box and told you that it contained something made by Michelangelo, because of his talent and creativity you would expect to find something of tremendous value in the box.

Similarly, the Bible is precious to those who know the Author, because we are aware of His tremendous ability and creativity. We expect more from His book, than do those who remain unrelated to Him and therefore unenlightened about Him, regardless of how intelligent they may be. In fact, the more we know of Him, His ability, His character, His power, His compassion, His goodness, His love the more expectation, or faith, we have to find blessings in His Word.

Seven Basic Premises

At the outset it is wise to establish some basic premises. I approach the Word of God with reverence and awe, for it is the Word of God. God's word is infallible, although men are not. Seven basic premises from which I operate are foundations upon which to base this search for truth.

Premise Number 1

Jesus Christ is the Wisdom of God. He is also the *Logos*, the Word of God and is therefore, Himself the object of our search.

But of him are ye in Christ Jesus, who of God is made unto us wisdom... 1 Cor. 1:30a

Christ the power of God, and the wisdom of God.
1 Cor. 1:24

Jesus is the key to all wisdom, because all things were created by Him, and by Him all things consist. Only a Creator knows all and perfectly understands all about His creation.

For by him were all things created, that are in heaven, and that are in earth, visible and invisible, whether they be thrones, or dominions, or principalities, or powers: all things were created by him, and for him: And he is before all things...that in all things he might have the preeminence. Col. 1:16-18b

In addition He is both the beginning and the end; our past and future are in His hands.

I am Alpha and Omega, the beginning and the ending, saith the Lord, which is, and which was, and which is to come, the Almighty. Rev. 1:8

The Apostle Paul, an extremely wise and gifted man, made a decision to focus on Jesus Christ.

For I determined not to know any thing among you, save Jesus Christ, and him crucified. 1 Cor. 2:2

As the passages from First Corinthians indicate, it is Jesus Christ we are seeking.

Premise Number 2

God's great underlying purpose in His Word **is to reveal Jesus Christ**, and to draw all men unto God. It is written that all creation testifies to Jesus Christ; certainly He will be the focus of His Word.

The heavens declare the glory of God; and the firmament showeth his handiwork. Psa. 19:1

For the invisible things of him from the creation of the world are clearly seen, being understood by the things that are made, even his eternal power and Godhead.
Rom. 1:20

Premise Number 3

God is totally good. He is totally and perfectly logical; often works in observable patterns; and He is certainly not the author of confusion, nor does He contradict Himself. He is totally good from every aspect and in every respect, as James confirms. Therefore, if we find He has given us only part of an answer to a puzzling passage of Scripture, then He must have the rest of the answer for us, we just have not discovered it.

Every good gift and every perfect gift is from above, and cometh down from the Father of lights, with whom is no variableness, neither shadow of turning. James 1:17

God is a giver of good gifts. Wisdom, knowledge and understanding are such gifts as seen in the following chapters.

Premise Number 4

The Word of God is true and contains truth, even if I do not yet fully understand it. God's truth is not limited by my limited understanding; my understanding only limits me. His truth was there in His Word before I was born, but it only becomes beneficial to me when I am able to receive, understand, and obey it.

Premise Number 5

Every word in the Word is important and significant. Each word is there in accordance with the will and wisdom of God. Therefore, not one of them should be overlooked. Each should be considered carefully. We can, thus, treat the Word of God as if it is an encoded-message to be deciphered.

By way of illustration: there is a familiar saying 'some people can't see the forest for the trees.' In other words they get too caught up in the little details to see the big picture. As a former prospector and someone who loves the American West, I have restated this saying from the opposite premise: Don't get so wrapped up in the sight of the mountains on the horizon that you miss the beautiful wildflowers at your feet. This thought is applicable to the situation at hand. Do not let the idea, or the importance, of the story being told cause you to overlook the significant details, which may hold amplifying clues to additional significance or symbolism.

In natural prospecting and mining, the geologist searches for clues on the surface such as an outcropping which may indicate a rich vein of gold lying hidden beneath the surface. In a similar fashion we may find clues in Scripture which cause us to seek God for answers, or to plunge deeper into study. For example, why are some of the Psalms written in acrostic form, alphabetic sequence? Why are certain details provided assuming none are given by chance? For example, why is the account of the woman with the flow of blood intertwined with the raising of Jairus' daughter? Why was the first healing interrupted by a second healing? Why does the Holy Spirit record that the woman had her condition for twelve years, and that Jairus' daughter was twelve years old? (There are no coincidences with

God.) Why are we told that Jesus' robe was woven in one piece from the top down and wasn't to be torn? Why did the High Priest rend his clothes when Jesus answered him? Any of these might be excellent starting points for searches of your own. Assume that the question which occurs to you about a passage of Scripture is the Holy Spirit's personal encouragement for you to seek further understanding.[3]

Premise Number 6

God deserves our reverence. He is Holy; His word is Holy. *The fear of God is the beginning of wisdom.* Because "fear" in this passage is "awe," we must approach the Word of God not only with humility, but also with reverence and respect. God the Father expects reverence for Jesus.

They will reverence my son. Mat. 21:37

Someone recently commented after visiting our little Thursday Night meeting, "It seems in most of the churches or prayer meetings I visit the things of God are taken lightly, almost as if for granted, and there is a lack of reverence. But I really feel reverence for God and for His Word here." I took that as a great compliment, and pray that we never lose our awe of God and holy reverence for Him, His Son, His Spirit and for His Word.

Premise Number 7

God's will is for us to know! God desires for us to know the truth, about Himself, the Godhead, especially

[3] If these stimulate your curiosity and you'd be interested in reading or hearing what the author has discovered, you might wish to write for a listing of available, books, tapes and special reports on subjects such as these.

about Jesus Christ; that is why the Word was made flesh; that is why the stone was rolled away from the empty tomb. Jesus could just as easily have walked through that stone, as He walked through the closed door of the upper room. The stone was rolled away in order that we might know that the tomb was empty and that He had risen from the dead.

Prospecting For Wisdom

On one occasion while prospecting with a friend in my youth, we came upon a long abandoned sapphire mine. Because the shafts and tunnels of the mine were either collapsed or unsafe, we had to content ourselves with working the tailings. We reworked some of the ore which had been dumped outside the shafts in huge piles after the original mining process. The miners had removed all the large and easily recoverable sapphires, but occasionally overlooked the more difficult to find smaller sapphires which required breaking the surrounding rock. Regrettably our success was minimal. I still have somewhere in an aspirin tin the results of all that particular week's effort: several stones too small to cut.

My goal is to stimulate within each believer a desire to study and to prospect for himself in the Word of God for the wisdom to be found within it. Some will respond to this teaching and discover a great love for the Truth and for the Word. These will then diligently apply their own effort to the task of digging deeply, mining, the Word for themselves. Some may tunnel, penetrating into the ground seeking new veins, others may seek those nuggets of gold which have been carried to the surface and are to be found in stream beds. Still others may be content to just work the tailings, satisfied with what others have already found, or brought to the surface. Would not a prospector be foolish indeed, if he refused to follow the exposed portion of a gold vein to the exceeding great riches to which it might lead him?

Having established that God desires for us to have His truth, where do we begin our search for wisdom?

In the beginning God. Gen. 1:1

Scripture begins with God and so must we. He is both the focal point and the starting point of all true wisdom, and we will discover that He is also the end result of all wisdom. As He is the Alpha and Omega, the beginning and the ending, the Author and Finisher of our faith, so also we will discover Him to be the beginning and the end of all wisdom.

Jesus was Co-Creator with God and by Him all things presently consist ("stand," "are established," "held together"). It is He who holds this earth together like glue, or gravity and it is by His power that this planet is held in its place and prevented from careening off to destruction in outer space.

That the God of our Lord Jesus Christ, the Father of glory, may give unto you the spirit of wisdom and revelation in the knowledge of him. Eph. 1:16b-17

This passage indicates that both revelation and wisdom are somehow related to knowledge of Jesus Christ. All of which leads to the first key to the door of the treasure house of knowledge, a key that can unlock all the wisdom and secrets of the universe. Jesus is not only the Wisdom of God, but also wisdom is hidden in Him:

To the acknowledgment of the mystery of God, and of the Father, and of Christ; In whom are hid all the treasures of wisdom and knowledge. 1Col. 2:2b-3

In Scripture a mystery is something previously hidden from the eyes of man, but which is revealed to the faithful in accordance with the will of God by the action of the Holy Spirit. The Spirit is revealing that there is a long hidden mystery, now revealed to the faithful by, or in, Jesus Christ.

Jesus Christ is truly All-in-All. He is the door to the treasure house of understanding; the Wisdom of God, the treasure which we are seeking; and He is the very treasure house itself, for it is "in Him" that the treasure of wisdom is to be found.

If we can accept the premise that Jesus Christ is indeed the divine, miraculously conceived, Son of God, whom God the Father promised to send in accordance with His will and plan from before the foundation of the present world, then it is not at all illogical to assume that He should be God's focus and that He wants us to fully understand all the truths concerning Him.

Since God has all knowledge, and we know He desires for us to know, How do we go about getting that knowledge? I don't pretend to have all the answers, but I have seven additional keys to offer which have worked effectively for me, and are akin to those utilized by Daniel, among the wisest of men, as he sought truth and understanding from God.

CHAPTER THREE

DANIEL, A PATTERN SEEKER AND OBTAINER OF WISDOM

When ye therefore shall see the abomination of desolation, spoken of by Daniel the prophet, stand in the holy place, (whoso readeth, let him understand.) Mat. 24:15

In this passage quoted from the Book of Daniel, the Lord Jesus Christ, Himself, placed His stamp of approval upon Daniel and the words which he recorded when He referred to him as *Daniel, the prophet.*

In the process of studying and teaching on this subject, I decided to base the teaching on truths which I discovered in the amazing book of Daniel. I decided to investigate Daniel as a pattern for successfully seeking God. Daniel was apparently, according to God Himself, *the wisest mortal* who ever lived, excluding Jesus Christ.

This statement requires substantiation since most would consider Solomon to have been the wisest, based upon God's statements in First Kings chapters three and four. Yet in a parallel passage Solomon's greatness is equated as it usually was in Jewish thought with *the riches and power* won by the utilization of wisdom.

Wisdom and knowledge is granted unto thee; and I will give thee riches, and wealth, and honour, such as none of the kings have had that have been before thee, neither shall there any after thee have the like. 2 Chr. 1:12

If Daniel was not the wisest, he was a close second to Solomon. Daniel was a godly man who was also considered among the three most righteous in the sight of God.

Though these three men, Noah, Daniel, and Job, were in it, they should deliver but their own souls by their righteousness, saith the Lord God. Ezek. 14:14

Because God could apparently find no wiser nor more righteous individual with which to contrast Satan, whom He addresses through the Prince of Tyrus, speaking facetiously, he uses Daniel.

Behold, thou art ***wiser than Daniel;*** *there is no secret that they can hide from thee.* Ezek. 28:3

God having said Daniel was one of the wisest and most righteous men who ever lived, perhaps we, too, can learn to receive wisdom from God by studying the methods which Daniel employed, and the principles he utilized in his own successful searches for wisdom from God.

Who Was Daniel?

Daniel was a contemporary of several other prophets of God: Ezekiel, Ezra, Jeremiah, and Zerubbabel. He lived from approximately 607 B.C. to at least 534 B.C. Like

Melchizedek, Daniel's birth and death are not recorded. His parents are not mentioned and the last angelic message to Daniel instructs him merely to *go his way till the end*. Dan 12:9.

His book is foundational to the New Testament, introducing doctrines, especially those concerning the end-time themes, such as "the times of the Gentiles" spoken of in Luke 21:24, the apostasy of the church, the manifesting of the man of sin, the period of "great tribulation," the Lord's second coming, the resurrections and the judgments, and numerous other symbolic foreshadowings.

Daniel was one of the most gifted of God's seers. He was a prophet (Heb. *nabi*). The Hebrew word indicates not primarily an office, but the prophet was rather a preacher of righteousness to the people of his day. His main task was to cause men to live righteously in light of the things which he foresaw and interpreted for them. He also warned his hearers of things to come if they failed to obey the will of God. The Hebrew root word (*naba*) not only carries the meaning of foretelling future events, but also means to pray and to make supplications. Thus, we often see the true prophet of God making intercession for the people, seeking the mercy of God for them.

Daniel served under some of the world's cruelest and most ruthless rulers. As an example, king Nebuchadnezzar was so ruthless, evil and hardened a ruler that he could "roast his enemies alive," as he almost did Shadrach, Meshach, and Abednego;

> *The Lord make thee like Zedekiah and like Ahab, whom the king of Babylon roasted in the fire;* Jer. 29:22

One of his most barbarous acts was to murder the twelve sons of a later Zedekiah, a king of Judah, before his eyes and then to blind the king, so that the last thing he would remember was the deaths of his sons.

And the king of Babylon slew the sons of Zedekiah before his eyes: he slew also all the princes of Judah in Riblah. Then he put out the eyes of Zedekiah; and the king of Babylon bound him in chains, and carried him to Babylon, and put him in prison till the day of his death.

Jer. 52:10-11

Daniel, on the other hand, is perhaps the only character in the Bible presented without a flaw in his character, who walked perfectly, meaning righteously, before His God, and who therefore serves as a proper "archetype" or foreshadowing of Jesus Christ, as chapter nine in this book, Revelation of Daniel Six, confirms.

Daniel was a man to whom astounding revelations were granted. His predictions were so amazing and so perfectly fulfilled, that many scholars and critics have attempted, unsuccessfully, to deny the authenticity of the book bearing his name.

How did he receive the truths which he obtained from God? What did Daniel do? What were his responsibilities? Were there methods which he employed, which we might also be able to use?

Daniel, I believe, was given to us by God to serve as a pattern. Daniel was an archetype foreshadowing Jesus Christ, the Messiah. Jesus Christ lived as an example of how to relate to and receive from God. Both prayed regularly and regularly received wisdom from God. Daniel also provides a pattern as a successful seeker of God.

Daniel, Our Pattern "Seeker"

Daniel, Chapter 1

What may we learn from Daniel, who as a child was carried away as a captive from his home and family into a foreign and pagan land?

And the king...[told]*...the master of his eunuchs, that he should bring certain of the children of Israel, and of the king's seed, and of the princes; Children in whom was no blemish, but well favoured, and skilful in all wisdom, and cunning in knowledge, and understanding science, and such as had ability in them to stand in the king's palace, and whom they might teach the learning and the tongue of the Chaldeans.* Dan. 1:3-4

The Hebrew children selected were already educated and had demonstrated their abilities, before being taken captive to Babylon. They were accomplished students. If Daniel's early learning seems intimidating, remember that learning can take place at any age. Even if one has not prepared, remember it's never too late for someone to start applying himself.

Now among these...the children of Judah, Daniel, Hananiah, Mishael, and Azariah: Unto whom the prince of the eunuchs gave names: for he gave unto Daniel the name of Belteshazzar; and to Hananiah, of Shadrach; and to Mishael, of Meshach; and to Azariah, of Abednego.
Dan. 1:6-7

Although a captive in a foreign land, Daniel decided to do his best to remain pure and uncorrupted by his environment.

But Daniel purposed in his heart that he would not defile himself...therefore he requested of the prince of the eunuchs that he might not defile himself. Dan. 1:8

God provides help for those who determine to deny themselves, either to please or serve God, for,

God is faithful, who will not suffer you to be tempted above that ye are able; but will with the temptation also make a way to escape. 1 Cor. 10:13

God prepared favor for him in the heart of the one to whom Daniel would appeal.

Now God had brought Daniel into favour and tender love with the prince of the eunuchs. Dan. 1:9

Prove thy servants, I beseech thee, ten days; and let them give us pulse to eat, and water to drink. Dan. 1:12

The polite refusal of Daniel and his friends to partake of the food of the king defiled by consecration to Babylonian idols, indicates the depth of their commitment and dedication to their God. Daniel and the others valued their relationship to God above their personal comfort or gratification with food. They fasted from the defiled foods, a partial fast, by eating only cereal, grains, and foods which grew naturally. They abstained from foods which had to be killed, which possessed blood and had been sacrificed, and wine which had to be fermented.[4]

Daniel was willing to put his complete trust in God to deliver him and his companions. Daniel put his faith to the test; he was not testing God, but rather was 'daring to step out of the boat,' like Peter walking on the water, by relying upon God's promises to preserve and protect those who trust in Him.

Thou wilt keep him in perfect peace, whose mind is stayed on thee: because he trusteth in thee. Isa. 26:3

Daniel and his three friends gave up food (i.e., a type of a partial fast) and, in turn, God gave to them, but you cannot out-give God.

As for these four children, God gave them knowledge and skill in all learning and wisdom: and Daniel had understanding in all visions and dreams. Dan. 1:17

Notice what they received was *given,* as gifts, by God.

And in all matters of wisdom and understanding, that the king inquired of them, he found them ten times better than all the magicians and astrologers that were in all his realm. Dan. 1:20

After a ten-day test the Hebrew children were ten times better than all the others in the court who relied upon both natural and occult power means, using the methods of the astrologers, magicians, sorcerers, Chaldeans and all other wise men.

[4] Daniel apparently abstained from meat and wine only temporarily, because he is seen again later in life (Daniel 10:3) fasting, eating no *bread...flesh nor wine.*

Summary

In the first chapter of Daniel God provided abundantly. Daniel's responsibilities were the sacrifices of study and self-discipline.

Daniel, Chapter 2

King Nebuchadnezzar soon had a dream which he could not remember, except that it was important, and so he demanded an interpretation from his staff of wise men, sorcerers, astrologers, and magicians. None, of course, could interpret or describe the *unremembered* dream. In fact they said:

It is a rare thing that the king requireth, and there is none other that can show it before the king, except the gods, whose dwelling is not with flesh. Dan. 2:11

Their inability angered the king. He became enraged and decreed death for all the wise men including Daniel and his friends, who were not present. When Daniel heard about it, he risked his life by promising to give the king the interpretation of the dream.

Then Daniel went in, and desired of the king that he would give him time, and that he would show the king the interpretation. Dan. 2:16

Daniel wasn't in a hurry. Using patience, he requested time from the king in which to seek God for the answer. Perhaps it was the result of a word of knowledge that he was able to promise the answer to the king's dream before he had it, or it could simply have been a statement of great faith.

Next, he obtained prayer support in like-minded agreement, from Shadrach, Meshach, and Abednego.

Then Daniel went to his house, and made the thing known to Hananiah, Mishael, and Azariah, his companions: That they would desire mercies of the God of heaven concerning this secret. Dan. 2:17

Daniel and his friends were properly motivated; they were praying as if their lives depended upon getting an answer from God, because they did. God has promised to be found when we seek after Him with wholehearted abandonment.

And ye shall seek me, and find me, when ye shall search for me with all your heart. Jer. 29:13

The opposite of wholehearted is double-minded. These four were not double-minded; they wanted, and needed, an answer.

Then was the secret revealed unto Daniel in a night vision. Dan. 2:19a

The answer came in a night vision. I'm sure Daniel was prayerfully seeking God for the answer. He may have been wakened from his sleep or the vision may have simply come to him while he was praying. What he was doing at the time isn't specified. Nonetheless, the answer came through a vision in the night.

Then Daniel blessed the God of heaven. Dan. 2:19b

Daniel was thankful. He did not take God's answer of mercy and grace for granted. All too frequently, Christians today, like the Jews of old, are not properly thankful, as illustrated in the story of the ten lepers.

Daniel gave God the glory; he was careful not to take any of it for himself. His thanks encompass four and one half verses to thank God for what had happened in the first half of verse 19.

Blessed be the name of God for ever and ever: for wisdom and might are his...he giveth wisdom unto the wise, and knowledge to them that know understanding that know understanding: Dan. 2:20-21

He revealeth the deep and secret things...I thank thee, and praise thee, O thou God of my fathers, who hast given me wisdom and might, and hast made known unto me now what we desired of thee. Dan. 2:22a,23a

The secret of the dream was revealed to Daniel and told to his friends *what we desired.* Daniel restates that wisdom and knowledge are gifts. (cf.1:17, 2:23, and 1 Cor. 12:8) Regrettably, some stumble even to this present day over the gifts of the Spirit and the possibility of secrets being revealed unto man by God, assuming that some things are meant to remain hidden. They are partially correct; it is true that,

The secret things belong unto the Lord our God: but those things which are revealed belong unto us and to our children for ever, that we may do all the words of this law. Deut. 29:29

When Daniel made the following statement he may have had a deeper meaning than we first expected.

For thou hast now made known unto us the king's matter.
Dan. 2:23b

He referred at least to the matter concerning King Nebuchadnezzar's forgotten dream. But perhaps he also referred to the revelation of a secret of the True King, Almighty God, which had been made known to Daniel.

Daniel answered in the presence of the king, and said, The secret which the king hath demanded cannot the wise men, the astrologers, the magicians, the soothsayers, show unto the king; But there is a God in heaven that revealeth secrets, and maketh known to the king Nebuchadnezzar what shall be in the latter days. Thy dream, and the visions of thy head upon thy bed, are these. Dan. 2:27-28

If God even gave a revelation to a gentile king, an unbeliever, a very evil man, upon his bed in a dream and night vision. How much more should we, who are His children, members of His family by blood, expect to hear from Him?

Thy dream, and the visions of thy head upon thy bed, are these. Dan. 2:28

Even this heathen king then realized and exclaimed,

Your God is...a revealer of secrets. Dan. 2:47

It is in accordance with God's very nature and generosity to give the answers to questions and to reveal secrets. King Nebuchadnezzar spoke truthfully when he agreed with what Daniel had said earlier, declaring a truth of which many modern Christians have lost sight.

But there is a God in heaven that revealeth secrets.

Dan. 2:28a

How did Daniel *know* that God was going to be "a revealer of secrets" when He declared to Nebuchadnezzar that God would reveal the forgotten dream? He no doubt based his belief upon the fact that God had in the past revealed secrets to His prophets.

Like our pattern, Daniel, we can also believe that what has been true of God in the past, what He has said or done is still true of Him today. Thus, if ever He was a revealer of truth, we know since He has said "I change not!", that He is still a revealer of truth! Never accept as fact, the statement which we so often hear, "You aren't meant to know," without first seeking God. Daniel, our pattern did not.

Summary

Daniel had complete faith in God's will to grant revelation.

Daniel, Chapter 3

Although Daniel is not mentioned in chapter three, a parenthetic reaffirmation of truths is seen in the actions of his friends. The three companions of Daniel were committed to their God and were willing to put their lives on the line, exemplifying the Scripture:

And they overcame him by the blood of the Lamb, and by the word of their testimony; and they loved not their lives unto the death. Rev. 12:11

Their faith, trust, and desire to obey their God took precedence over their personal safety. They were sold out to God. No risk, or sacrifice undertaken in the Lord's service goes unnoticed by the Lord. Consider the following which came to me as a revelation, or as a God-inspired insight. We know, from passages such as John 19:30 and Hebrews 1:3 that the Lord Jesus Christ has finished all His necessary work, and is seated at the right hand of the Father, the Majesty on high. However, when Stephen was being stoned, Jesus was seen *standing.*

He, being full of the Holy Ghost, looked up stedfastly into heaven, and saw the glory of God, and Jesus standing on the right hand of God. Acts 7:55

Jesus was standing because one of His own followers was undergoing persecution for the Word's sake, for his faith in Jesus, and was so **vitally interested, the Lord Jesus Christ was on His feet, cheering Stephen on to victory!**

The three Hebrew children were not alone either in their time of trial. Someone was right there with them in the fiery furnace, seen even by the wicked king who had them thrown into the furnace.

He... said, Lo, I see four men loose, walking in the midst of the fire, and they have no hurt; and the form of the fourth is like the Son of God. Dan. 3:25

Summary

God extends His loving hand of protection to those who run risks for Him, who hold fast to His revelations.

Daniel, Chapter 4

The fourth chapter of Daniel is without question, the most unusual book in the Scripture, because it is the only entire chapter of the Bible written by a gentile. It is a decree of King Nebuchadnezzar, in which he relates another dream, and the thoughts and vision which Daniel interpreted for him.

The gentile king by his own testimony had dreams and saw visions in his head (mind), as did Daniel. They both wondered, and posed questions in their minds concerning the future. Both received answers while seeking God in bed in the night season, although Daniel's answers came while he meditated upon His God, and sought God for what needed to be revealed, and the things that were to come.

This matter is by the decree of the watchers, and the demand by the word of the holy ones: to the intent that the living may know that the most High ruleth in the kingdom of men, and giveth it to whomsoever he will, and setteth up over it the basest of men. Dan. 4:17

The angels, the "watchers" and "holy ones," operating within the will of God, confirm by their actions that it is the will of God for man to understand God's authority and will!

Summary

It is amazing that King Nebuchadnezzar grasps that Daniel's God is preeminent; the Most high God rules the affairs of men. In addition, God offers supernatural and sometimes angelic confirmation of His will to reveal truth and give understanding.

Daniel, Chapter 5

In the fifth chapter of Daniel a great feast was given by Belshazzar, a successor to Nebuchadnezzar. The finger of God wrote a message upon the wall which none could interpret. The writing caused the king great fear. Although Daniel was unknown to the king, he was recommended by the queen as one *in whom is the spirit of the holy gods...light and understanding and wisdom, like the wisdom of the gods*. He was summoned and offered riches and authority if he could interpret the writing.

Then Daniel answered and said before the king, Let thy gifts be to thyself, and give thy rewards to another; yet I will read the writing unto the king, and make known to him the interpretation. Dan. 5:17

Daniel refused to commercialize upon the gifts of God. He was not a prophet for profit. He rejected the king's offered reward, literally "a fee" in Hebrew.

He had such confidence in God, that he immediately promised to give the interpretation. Daniel must have recognized, that because God wastes no effort, and does nothing without a purpose, He would not have written a message that was not intended to be understood.[5]

Daniel boldly proclaimed righteousness to an unrighteous king. He spoke the prophetic interpretation of the writing, that Belshazzar had been judged and found wanting, and that his kingdom would be taken from him and given to the Medes and Persians. Before the sun rose the next morning, all had come to pass.

Summary

Daniel refused to commercialize upon the revelation from God, yet, boldly proclaimed it.

Daniel, Chapter 6

In chapter six, a most amazing and prophetic chapter, Daniel is described as faithful to God and to man, without "error or fault" towards either. (See chapter nine) Daniel's enemies recognized that because of his righteousness there could be no valid basis of accusation, and so they devised to "*find it against him concerning the law of his God.*" (Dan. 6:5) Even his enemies recognized his faithfulness, and the regularity of his prayers.

The false accusations of the evil men to King Darius was that he "regardeth not thee." (cf. 6:13, 3:12). Satan isn't very creative: uses the same old lies and temptations over and over: gold, girls, glory (pride).

In spite of the danger, Daniel chose to obey God rather

[5] This same logic prompted me to write the book *The Heavens Declare...* The Lord showed me the key to David's statement that the Lord named and numbered the stars. *He telleth the number of the stars; he calleth them all by their names.* Psa. 147:4

than man. His faith placed his relationship with God above personal safety, and he continued praying even when he knew that there was a contract out on his life for doing so.

Now when Daniel knew that the writing was signed, he went into his house; and his windows being open in his chamber toward Jerusalem, he kneeled upon his knees three times a day, and prayed, and gave thanks before his God, as he did aforetime. Dan. 6:10

Daniel, like Jesus whom he foreshadows, prayed regularly and consistently. The prayer life of both men, influenced their associates and affected their enemies. Daniel was a guiding force in the lives of the Hebrew children and an inspiration to all the faithful among the captives.

This chapter contains the characteristics of Daniel's personal prayer program: He had (1) a private place of prayer; (2) a posture of prayer, kneeling, (3) a purpose - (made his petition with thanksgiving) (4) a pattern: it was his persistent practice, "his custom" (5) a priority for praying, even at the risk of his life (6) peacefulness was his; he enjoyed peace and intimacy with God, and as a result, he (7) persevered and prevailed in prayer and God rewarded him with a mighty miracle of deliverance.

When Daniel was saved and vindicated "with signs and wonders following," he explained the reason.

My God hath sent his angel, and hath shut the lions' mouths, that they have not hurt me: forasmuch as before him innocency was found in me; and also before thee, O king, have I done no hurt. Dan. 6:22

Summary

Daniel did not allow intimidation to interfere with his spiritual life. He maintained his righteousness and kept himself blameless before man and God.

Daniel, Chapter 7

In the first year of Belshazzar king of Babylon Daniel had a dream and visions of his head upon his bed: then he wrote the dream, and told the sum of the matters. Dan. 7:1

Daniel had a dream and visions in the night and then wrote the dream and shared it with others.

After this I saw in the night visions Dan. 7:7a

Visions, or other revelations of truth, often come in installments as these did to Daniel in 7:1 and 7:7, which makes perseverance so important.

I considered the horns...I beheld till the thrones. Dan. 7:8,9

Daniel not only saw in his night vision, but also considered that which he saw; he pondered and mediated upon the truths revealed unto him. He didn't stop there; he beheld, kept on looking, until the revelation was completed.

Then having done what he could do, he sought supernatural enlightenment.

I...asked...So he told me, and made me know the interpretation of the things. Dan. 7:16

After receiving the interpretation of his vision, he faithfully continued pursuing truth and understanding.

Hitherto is the end of the matter. As for me, Daniel, my cogitations much troubled me, and my countenance changed in me: but I kept the matter in my heart.

Dan. 7:28

He considered and kept the matter in his heart, just as Mary kept the secret things revealed unto her in her heart, pondering them.

But Mary kept all these things, and pondered them in her heart. Luke 2:19

Summary

Daniel meditated upon these things, in his heart, rather than making a premature proclamation of the revelation.

Daniel, Chapter 8

Daniel had another vision and once again sought for its meaning.

And it came to pass, when I, even I Daniel, had seen the vision, and sought for the meaning. Dan. 8:15a.

Daniel sought the meaning of the vision, indicating he had a question in his heart and mind for which he was seeking the Lord for an answer, for interpretation, for understanding.

Then, behold, there stood before me as the appearance of a man. Dan. 8:15b

Having sought, the answer came to him in the form of a man to explain the answer. One, whom I assume to be the Lord Jesus Christ, appeared and commanded Gabriel to give the vision's interpretation unto Daniel.

And I heard a man's voice...which called, and said, Gabriel, make this man to understand the vision.

Dan. 8:16

Then Daniel heard a voice which instructed Gabriel to make him understand the vision. There is extreme significance for us in this passage: Not only is God's will for man to understand expressed tangibly in the presence of the angel Gabriel, but we also hear His instruction to Gabriel to make Daniel understand. The burden is upon the angel to cause Daniel to understand, not for Daniel to struggle to grasp God's truth!

Gabriel is commanded by God to give understanding to Daniel! This liberating truth takes away all the fear of missing God and the pressure that we must struggle and sweat to come to understand God's truth. (See God is a Perfect Communicator in chapter five.)

Then,

He [Gabriel] *said unto me, Understand, O son of man.... for at the time of the end shall be the vision.* Dan. 8:17

Those words of command spoken to Daniel, could as well be spoken to each of us today; *son of man, understand*!

Now as he was speaking with me, I was in a deep sleep on my face toward the ground: but he touched me, and set me upright. Dan. 8:18

Daniel was once again in a state of sleep when God's truth came to him. Perhaps God has to bypass human resistance to new truth by putting the conscious mind into a state of sleep so he can speak new truths into men's hearts and understanding. The angel then picked up Daniel, making him stand upright.

And he said, Behold, I will make thee know. Dan. 8:19

Again the burden was upon Gabriel, and he accepted it fully, promising to *make thee know*!

And I Daniel fainted, and was sick certain days; afterward I rose up, and did the king's business; and I was astonished at the vision, but none understood it. Dan. 8:27

Strangely, Daniel did not have full understanding of the vision even though it had been angelically explained to him. Obviously he understood only the portion that was appropriate for him at that time. Daniel certainly could not have comprehended the style of life that exists in our day, the day to which the prophecy in the vision referred.

Man cannot acquire all knowledge or all wisdom, for these remain resident with the source of all wisdom and knowledge, God the Father. (cf. Mat. 24:36) In the list of the gifts of the Spirit presented in I Corinthians 12, a word of wisdom and a word of knowledge, but not all of wisdom or knowledge, is to be imparted to the Spirit-endowed brethren.

Summary

God will give only as much revelation as we can comprehend and understand.

Daniel, Chapter 9

In the first year of his reign I, Daniel, understood by books the number of the years, whereof the word of the Lord came to Jeremiah the prophet, that he would accomplish seventy years in the desolations of Jerusalem. Dan. 9:2

Within the first verses of chapter nine is another technique Daniel used to seek answers from God. He discovered in books how many years it would be until Jerusalem was to be destroyed; but he wanted to know more; thus, he once again had a question upon his heart for God. He spells out his plan for obtaining the answer from God in verses three and four:

And I set my face unto the Lord God, to seek by prayer and supplications, with fasting, and sackcloth, and ashes: And I prayed unto the Lord my God, and made my confession, and said, O Lord, the great and dreadful God, keeping the covenant and mercy to them that love him, and to them that keep his commandments. Dan. 9:3-4

Here Daniel listed the seven steps which he employed on this occasion:

1.) He **set his face** (i.e., set his will; he determined to get the answer from God.) This used to be referred to among Christians as praying through. Daniel, like Jacob who wrestled all night with the angel, determined that he was going to get an answer from God.

2.) **He prayed**

3.) **He supplicated**, literally he implored, beseeched, humbly made petition.

4.) **He fasted,** abstaining from food, to bring his

body into subjection to his soul under his spirit; to attune his spiritual sensitivity.

5.) **He dressed in sackcloth**, humbling himself with slight discomfort; the roughness of his apparel served as an additional reminder of his prayer commitment.

6.) **He applied ashes**, which had a self-humbling effect, but also served as a public, or visible sign to others of his dedication to his task.

7.) **He** then **made his confession**, confessing on behalf of himself and his nation their collective failure to properly follow and obey God.

Daniel based his approach upon God's faithfulness as a covenant-keeping and merciful God. He observed correctly that Israel's failure to be blessed was a result of rebelling, departing from God's precepts and judgments, and for not hearkening to His prophets.

Daniel suggested repentance as a solution by turning from their iniquities.

As it is written in the law of Moses, all this evil is come upon us: yet made we not our prayer before the Lord our God, that we might turn from our iniquities, and understand thy truth. Dan. 9:13

He based God's hearing his prayer upon repentance:

Now therefore, O our God, hear the prayer of thy servant, and his supplications, and cause thy face to shine upon thy sanctuary that is desolate, for the Lord's sake. Dan. 9:17

O my God, incline thine ear, and hear; open thine eyes, and behold our desolations, and the city which is called by

thy name: for we do not present our supplications before thee for our righteousnesses, but for thy great mercies.
Dan. 9:18

Daniel approached God, not on the basis of the nation's righteousness, but on the basis (for the sake) of His own righteousness (provided to us in Jesus Christ), and for the sake of His great mercy!

And whiles I was speaking, and praying, and confessing my sin and the sin of my people Israel, and presenting my supplication before the Lord my God for the holy mountain of my God. Dan. 9:20

While Daniel was still praying, before he even thought he had said enough, God sent the answer. (See what happened even before Peter could give an altar call in Acts 10:44.) So significant was this point that he repeated it, and this verse is one of the greatest faith-building passages in Scripture if we can only grasp it:

Yea, whiles I was speaking in prayer, even the man Gabriel, whom I had seen in the vision at the beginning, being caused to fly swiftly, touched me about the time of the evening oblation. Dan. 9:21

Gabriel was caused to fly swiftly, to speedily deliver the answer at the time of the evening sacrifice. Why? There was no hurry; the fulfillment was far in the future, except that God desired to promptly bless with answers the man who seeks him. Prayer brings results and Daniel saw the connection.

And he informed me, and talked with me, and said, O Daniel, I am now come forth to give thee skill and understanding. Dan. 9:22

The heavenly visitor Gabriel, explained his speedy arrival was necessary to give Daniel skill and understanding. The exciting element was that the answer arrived while Daniel was still praying. While he was speaking, praying, confessing, and presenting his supplications, even before he had finished his prayer, God dispatched His messenger Gabriel with the answer to Daniel's unfinished prayer!

At the beginning of thy supplications the commandment came forth, and I am come to show thee; for thou art greatly beloved: therefore understand the matter, and consider the vision. Dan. 9:23

At the beginning of his prayer, as Daniel started to pray, God already knew the desire of his heart to be understanding and He granted it.

How it blesses my heart to see what God is telling us here: at the beginning of Daniel's prayer the commandment came forth. At the very moment Daniel set his heart to understand, God dispatched Gabriel with the answer. It was not a suggestion or a request, but a commandment that God gave to Gabriel to show [to manifest, announce, explain] the truth to Daniel!

In the above passage, Daniel was addressed as greatly beloved. Most translators have rendered the Hebrew word *chamad*, delight in, desire, greatly beloved, precious, and a goodly lust, assuming God is the source of action. It is a beautiful thought that God could love a human, such as Daniel, with the same kind of love with which He spoke of

His own Beloved Son. However, if the source of action is assumed to be the subject, Daniel, it might be properly rendered, as A. B. Simpson did, "man of great desires," and "greatly devoted." Daniel certainly was a man of great desire, who faithfully devoted himself to obtaining truth from God. He delighted and desired what was precious and lusted in a good way for that which was precious, wisdom from God.

This alternative rendering is significant from the standpoint of our faith, lest we believe that Daniel was loved more by the Father than we might be, and therefore was uniquely eligible for wisdom because he was an especially favored son.

Gabriel again made it clear to Daniel that he was commanded to give him understanding. When God sent His messenger and told him to give understanding, it was a commandment to do so, and the commandment also included making sure that the one hearing understands, as He stated in 8:16, *make this man to understand the vision.* So the dispatching also included causing the one hearing to understand that which was communicated.

It is possible to see and not perceive; to hear and not understand (Mark 4:12a). To not to be able to perceive, or to hear and understand God, His will, His Word, His ways is a judgment of blindness from God, as Jesus warned:

Therefore speak I to them in parables: because they seeing see not; and hearing they hear not, neither do they understand. And in them is fulfilled the prophecy of Esaias, which saith, By hearing ye shall hear, and shall not understand; and seeing ye shall see, and shall not perceive: But blessed are your eyes, for they see: and your ears, for they hear. Mat. 13:14,16

It is also possible to understand and yet not consider, as Gabriel states in the last phrase of verse twenty-three. Daniel was specifically directed by Gabriel after he was given understanding, to also consider the vision and his new insight to it. Clearly it is not enough to have understanding, one must also do something with the understanding granted, in this case consider, view wisely and carefully.

This condition of understanding while not considering unfortunately describes the state of most modern Christians. Many of us have been blessed to understand the basics of Christianity and its message, but have become complacent. We have become satisfied with the status-quo; we have ceased to hunger for the things of God. Thus, many are guilty of departing from the intensity of our "first love," mentioned in Revelation.

Summary

This chapter illustrates the eagerness of God to provide answers to Daniel's inquiries, to respond to his praying.

Daniel, Chapter 10

In the third year of Cyrus king of Persia a thing was revealed unto Daniel, whose name was called Belteshazzar; and the thing was true, but the time appointed was long: and he understood the thing, and had understanding of the vision. Dan. 10:1

What was revealed was not specified as a dream or a vision but was, nonetheless, a revelation to Daniel from the heart and mind of God.

In those days I Daniel was mourning three full weeks. I ate no pleasant bread, neither came flesh nor wine in my mouth, neither did I anoint myself at all, till three whole weeks were fulfilled. Then I lifted up mine eyes, and looked, and behold a certain man clothed in linen, whose loins were girded with fine gold of Uphaz: His body also was like the beryl, and his face as the appearance of lightning, and his eyes as lamps of fire, and his arms and his feet like in colour to polished brass, and the voice of his words like the voice of a multitude. Dan. 10:2-6

Daniel, determined to seek the Lord for information, put himself on a partial fast similar to his ten-day fast of chapter two. However, this fast continued for twenty-one days.

And I Daniel alone saw the vision: for the men that were with me saw not the vision; but a great quaking fell upon them, so that they fled to hide themselves. Dan. 10:7

On the twenty-first day he had a vision of a man. Daniel's experience was similar to that of Paul in Acts, chapter 9. Like Paul, Daniel alone saw the vision; the men with him did not.

Therefore I was left alone, and saw this great vision, and there remained no strength in me...Yet heard I the voice of his words: and when I heard the voice of his words, then was I in a deep sleep on my face, and my face toward the ground. Dan. 10:8a,9

Daniel, overpowered by the Presence, found himself on the ground on his face before the Man seen in the vision.

And, behold, an hand touched me, which set me upon my knees and upon the palms of my hands. And he said unto me, O Daniel, a man greatly beloved, understand the words that I speak unto thee, and stand upright: for unto thee am I now sent. And when he had spoken this word unto me, I stood trembling. Dan. 10:10-11

This vision has confused some readers. I believe the reason for the confusion is that there are two supernatural heavenly beings present, both of whom are seen in the vision. The first is the One I assume to be the Lord Jesus Christ, who is described in verses five and six, and whose voice sounds like a multitude. When Daniel heard His voice, his own strength departed from him and he found himself prostrated on the ground in a deep sleep before this Being.

Next the hand of an *angel*, probably Gabriel, as in chapters eight and nine, touched Daniel and lifted him to a hands-and-knees position. When the angel spoke to him, he told him to stand.

An angel, even the angel Gabriel, would not receive prostrate worship, nor would the Lord Jesus Christ have been given a commandment to enlighten Daniel. The one speaking in verse ten, could not have been the Lord Jesus Christ, whom I believe was seen in the vision in verses 2-6. Jesus would have been the Sender of messenger angels, and certainly could not have been resisted for even one day, much less twenty-one, by a mere demonic territorial prince.

Daniel has progressed from his past experience. Previously he was set upright upon his feet by the angel's power, but now his role is expanded, more is expected of him, and he is required to stand up on his own power. Daniel is growing.

In both cases Daniel was in a trance and prostrated face down before the presence of Jesus. Yet this time, he was told to *understand* what I say and *stand up*.

Believers today will find it easier to stand as commanded in the sixth chapter of Ephesians if we, like Daniel, understand the sixth chapter of Ephesians. (See The Whole Armour of God in the Appendix.)

The progression in Daniel's methods of seeking truth from God illustrates how God stretches all of us. He expects us to grow and develop. For example during the honeymoon stage of my walk with him and my early experiences with prayer, it often seemed as if no sooner did I get the requests out of my mouth than the answers arrived. But then there came a point when the answer was delayed, a period of time elapsed between the point of praying and when the answer arrived. This caused my faith to mature. Naturally, it takes no faith to receive something immediately; faith awaits the fulfillment of the promise.

God expects more of us as we grow, in the same way we, as parents, treat a child differently at different ages. We may give our one-year old a glass of water as soon as he cries. Hopefully we are not treating that child the same when he is ten or twelve. At that age we expect him to either ask politely for a glass of water, or to get it for himself. If we continue treating the child at ten or twelve as we did when he was one, he will remain immature, infantile, and be handicapped.

Then said he unto me, Fear not, Daniel: for from the first day that thou didst set thine heart to understand, and to chasten thyself before thy God, thy words were heard, and I am come for thy words. Dan. 10:12

The angel Gabriel repeats a faith-building statement similar to the one made in chapter 9:23a, *At the beginning of thy supplications the commandment came forth, and I am come to show thee...* Now, he says *from the first day.*

Daniel was told that from the very first day, or moment, that he set his heart to seek understanding from God, his prayer was heard, immediately; and the answer was dispatched immediately. That is fantastic but it gets even better. Do you see the other great faith-building truth in this verse? Gabriel says, *I am come for thy words.* An astounding thought, that the words of man can move heaven and cause an angel as important as Gabriel to be dispatched.

Consider the implications: our words can move heaven! God hears our words spoken in prayer and immediately dispatches the answer to any proper prayer, as the New Testament confirms:

And this is the confidence that we have in him, that, if we ask any thing according to his will, he heareth us: And if we know that he hear us, whatsoever we ask, we know that we have the petitions that we desired of him.

1 John 5:14-15

However, Gabriel explained the delay in responding to his request for understanding, on this occasion was due to satanic opposition presented by the demonic ruling prince over the country of Persia.

But the prince of the kingdom of Persia withstood me one and twenty days: but, lo, Michael, one of the chief princes, came to help me; and I remained there with the kings of Persia. Dan. 10:13

The Holy Spirit has given this explanation for delayed answers to our prayer requests: it can be due to satanic opposition. For this reason, perseverance is extremely important.

Now I am come to make thee understand what shall befall thy people in the latter days: for yet the vision is for many days. Dan. 10:14

For the third time in Daniel, Gabriel must make him know. After reading this in 8:16 and 9:25, the reader must recognize a recurring theme in Daniel: God sends angels to make man understand. However, even though Daniel was made to understand the vision with heavenly help, it was for the distant future. Many modern pharisees, legalists and heresy hunters would have called for the stoning of Daniel, because the prophecies he wrote did not come to pass within his lifetime. Many today consider the infallible test of the validity of a prophecy to be "does it come to pass?" (i.e., within a time frame which they are able to judge.) This observation is not intended by any means to give a blanket endorsement of all modern prophecy; all must be tested and judged as Paul advised in First Corinthians 2:15;14:29.

It is exciting to see the next promise made by the angel and endorsed, in essence, by the Holy Spirit who caused it to be recorded.

I will show thee that which is noted in the scripture of truth.
Dan. 10:21

The angel promised in this verse, once again, to explain the Scriptures. This promise is certainly a faith builder because it also underscores that there is more to the

Scripture than just the surface meaning of the words. Based on verse 21, we pray.

-- Our Prayer --

Lord, again we give You praise, for You are the revealer of secrets, and we pray that to us also, You, by Your Spirit will show...that which is noted in the scripture of truth.

Summary

Revelation is received by perseverance through fasting and self-humbling.

Daniel, Chapter 11

After being strengthened by angels on at least three occasions, a measure of the progressive growth of Daniel is observed when he strengthened King Darius.

Also I in the first year of Darius the Mede, even I, stood to confirm and to strengthen him. Dan 11:1

Paul described such activity in the New Testament.

[God] *Who comforteth us in all our tribulation, that we may be able to comfort them which are in any trouble, by the comfort wherewith we ourselves are comforted of God.*
2 Cor. 1:4

Daniel in turn did for Darius, what the angelic beings in the past had done for him. He explained the future, had a heart to help, was enabled to do so, and shared the knowledge which he had received.

Summary

The purpose of the revelation is ministry to others, and personal encouragement.

Daniel, Chapter 12

The book of Daniel closes with wisdom in a prophetic description of our day.

But thou, O Daniel, shut up the words, and seal the book, even to the time of the end: many shall run to and fro, and knowledge shall be increased. Dan. 12:4

Today worldly knowledge is indeed being increased. By virtue of computers in this information age man's accumulated knowledge is expanding exponentially. For example, it has been reported that a current Sunday edition of the New York times contains more information than a person in Thomas Jefferson's day could accumulate in a lifetime. However, even as there is an outpouring from the tree of knowledge, there is also available a corresponding outpouring of God's wisdom from Jesus, the Tree of Life.

And I heard, but I understood not: then said I, O my Lord, what shall be the end of these things? Dan. 12:8

In the last view of Daniel, the aged prophet was still seeking information from His God. His final recorded words were yet asking another question of His God. In fact, questioning became a way of life, a means of staying in direct communication with God. One learns to continually seek answers from God, especially about His ways, His will or His Word.

The final passages of the book bearing his name contain another divine promise concerning the acquisition of wisdom:

But the wise shall understand. Dan. 12:10

Summary

A glorious promise of insight given to Daniel is extended to future believing seekers of wisdom. As this age draws to a close, those same gifts of revelation are becoming more relevant since His coming is close, this promise is surely for today.

The principles noted in each chapter of the writings of Daniel, are

1 God rules that sacrifice and self-discipline precede revelation.

2 God is clearly willing to grant revelation.

3 God stands beside those who fully seek Him.

4 God offers supernatural confirmation of His truth.

5 God upon occasion requires revelation to be freely and boldly proclaimed.

6 God calls us to resist intimidation.

7 God leads us to proclaim the truths given in His timing.

8 God gives only the measure of truth which we are able to grasp at the time.

9 God is eager to manifest His truth to us.

10 God sometimes requires perseverance in prayer and fasting to break the satanic opposition to His truth being revealed.

11 God grants revelation for the benefit of His people.

12 God promises to continue granting revealed truth until the end to those who would be wise.

Christian, if you want to receive insights into Heaven, and revelations about the workings of the kingdom of God, or the meaning of God's word, as Daniel did; if you want to open an even more powerful channel to God than that which you now enjoy, I suggest you consider utilizing the seven keys, described in the next chapter.

-- Our Prayer --

O God, Grantor of all wisdom, we pray that we, each reader and I, may be numbered among those who are wise, and who shall understand. Just as You have promised!

CHAPTER FOUR

SEVEN KEYS TO RECEIVE ANSWERS FROM GOD

Each of the seven keys has practical applications and may be used by any believer. Apply each of them fully in a coordinated manner, as Daniel did, and successfully receive God's wisdom.

KEY 1 The key to receiving truth from God and gaining understanding in His Word is to ask! To obtain an answer from God, you must have a question.

KEY 2 Pose your question of God at night.

KEY 3 Seek an answer whole-heartedly

KEY 4 God requires you to R O H R
Repentance, obedience, holiness, and righteousness.

KEY 5 Submit fully to the Teacher.

KEY 6 Apply yourself; become a student.

KEY 7 Meditate creatively.

Wisdom is the Result of a Question

Seek ye the Lord while he may be found, call ye upon him while he is near. Isa. 55:6

Ask, and it shall be given you; seek, and ye shall find; knock, and it shall be opened unto you. Mat. 7:7

One thing have I desired of the Lord, that will I seek after; that I may dwell in the house of the Lord all the days of my life, to behold the beauty of the Lord, and to inquire in his temple. Psa. 27:4

And they that know thy name will put their trust in thee: for thou, Lord, hast not forsaken them that seek thee.
Psa. 9:10

They that seek the Lord understand all things. Prov. 28:5

KEY 1 **ASK QUESTIONS OF GOD**

For God to give an answer, we must have a question. Sometimes this is a conscious process; sometimes it may be unconscious. We may not even be aware that we are seeking God, which is why some people seem to get answers without even being aware of asking a question. They have had a matter on their hearts for so long they have even forgotten asking the question. Naturally, it is also possible for God to sovereignly give an unsought revelation. But Daniel, in each instance, had a question on his heart.

Many people have told me they have never heard from God. If there is one complaint more than any other I have heard in the last twenty-five years in my prayer room, it is that "God doesn't speak to me."

Although it may seem terribly obvious, one of the most important keys in this area I can share with you is that in order for God to tell you something you desire to know, *you must have a question!* You must have asked, or be asking, something of Him for Him to be able to give you *an answer.*

I acknowledge there can be instances when God may choose to sovereignly reveal things, or even Himself, to people who are not consciously seeking Him. Saul, as an example, on the road to Damascus was "apprehended" by Jesus Christ, unaware, until that moment that he was in conflict with the will of God. Yet, grace was extended to him and he *obtained mercy, because I did it ignorantly in unbelief.* 1 Tim. 1:13b

I believe that God deeply desires to answer our questions, to respond to our seeking Him, but we need a link. He could, of course, just pour out wisdom upon us unsolicited, but if He did, we probably would not believe it. We would assume that it was just something we thought up.

A question is a link, a conduit, between the seen and unseen realms.

How Do We Do It?

What technique should be used to draw upon the vast storehouse of God's wisdom? He has made it simple and obvious. The key to getting truth from God is to ask, to have a question. But how are we to ask? James chapter, one offers another clue and encouragement.

If any of you lack wisdom, let him ask of God...and it shall be given him. James 1:5

These wise words of James, hold both the promise and the scriptural basis for expecting to receive God's wisdom. *Ask of God and it shall be given!* However, James adds both a caveat and a warning. We must ask expecting to receive.

But let him ask in faith, nothing wavering. For he that wavereth is like a wave of the sea driven with the wind and tossed. For let not that man think that he shall receive any thing of the Lord. James 1:6-7

Any man who doubts either that God will speak or give wisdom to him, might as well save his breath and not bother asking. Rather than being a negative, this is a tremendously positive scriptural promise. It is not limited by our merit, intelligence or worthiness. It is only predicated upon our asking in faith, which encourages our desire to search and seek.

An answer from God presupposes you have a question. You must have a question on your heart; you must have a question in order to tap into God's wisdom!

Yet ye have not, because ye ask not. James 4:2

Some men have no questions, like the Pharisee in Luke 18:10 who went to the temple to pray but left without uttering a single word of true prayer. He merely bragged about his own righteous acts and came away without receiving anything from the Lord, because he asked for nothing! The Publican, who had the proper credentials, a broken and contrite spirit, was seeking mercy for his own sinful state, received and *went down to his house justified.*

The Pharisee's situation is similar to that of the elder brother in the parable of the prodigal son. He complained that he didn't have even a young goat to roast for a party with his friends. His loving father replied, *all that I have is thine.* Luke 15:31 Had he asked he could have had, for the entire herd and the remaining estate were already his.

One evening as I was about to teach upon this subject a prophecy came forth which included the following personalized paraphrase of the words of James:

Draw nigh to me (God), and I (He) will draw nigh to you
James 4:8a

God confirmed His truth and my teaching of it in that meeting: as we seek God He will be found by us.

HELPFUL TECHNIQUE -- **Live it**

If you have a question about a passage of Scripture, prayerfully ask God to give you understanding and keep reading and meditating upon the passage. Personalize it, attempt to put yourself into the situation, try to mentally live it. All the while turn the account around in your mind, and allow God to show you possible variations of what might have actually occurred in the situation He described.

Don't be impatient, or expect to get everything there is to know about a particular passage all at once. I sought Him for years on certain passages, such as the intertwined healing accounts of the woman with the flow of blood and the raising of Jairus' daughter before gaining understanding.

Asking questions of God was a characteristic practice of Daniel. Many other heroes of the faith also posed questions to God.

Jesus Asked Questions

Jesus, our supreme pattern, as a man of prayer, began asking questions at an early age.

And when he [Jesus] *was twelve years old, they went up to Jerusalem after the custom of the feast. And it came to pass, that after three days they found him in the temple, sitting in the midst of the doctors, both hearing them, and asking them questions. And all that heard him were astonished at his understanding and answers.*

Luke 2:42,46-47

Then His frantic parents finally found him,

And when they saw him, they were amazed: and his mother said...[we]*...have sought thee sorrowing. And he said unto them, How is it that ye sought me?* [knew] *ye not that I must be about MY FATHER'S BUSINESS?*

Luke 2:48-49

Clearly, Jesus employed the same learning techniques which Daniel employed. He was asking questions of God which He referred to as being about His Father's business. By virtue of His admonition to His parents, He indicated that asking questions concerning the things of God was a natural part of the business of the Kingdom.

Even when He prayed *if it be thy will* in the Garden of Gethsemane, it was in the form of a question, although He anticipated and accepted the answer in advance.

The Disciples Asked Questions of The Lord

The actions of Jesus' Disciples offer another Scriptural pattern. A spokesman for the disciples asked Jesus, *Lord, teach us to pray, as John also taught his disciples.* Luke 11:1

The disciples knew that Jesus was evidently getting something from His praying they were not: He was communicating. They recognized their prayers were somehow inadequate. They knew they were not communicating the same way Jesus was. Their request implied they knew prayer is communication which indicates conversation, with both parties speaking *and hearing each other.*

How did Jesus' disciples learn? They were able to ask questions of God in person; they had access to the heart and mind of God, in Christ Jesus! Just as Jesus asked questions of the doctors of the Law when He was twelve, His own inner circle was able to ask questions of Him in person, as they often did concerning His teaching.

His disciples asked him concerning the parable.

Mark 7:17

We, similarly, have access today to the heart and mind of God via Jesus Christ with the aid of the Holy Spirit, whose ongoing ministry is to help believers discover God's truth.

If any of you lack wisdom, let him ask of God, that giveth to all liberally, and upbraideth not; and it shall be given him.
James 1:5

This is a present promise for us, and also foreshadows that fuller and more perfect knowing which will one day be ours when we shall "no longer see through a glass, darkly, but,"

Face to face: now I know in part; but then shall I know even as also I am known. 1 Cor. 13:12

One day we shall know perfectly, completely, and will know Him fully when we meet Him face to face. But for now He has promised that we can have wisdom, if we will but ask.

Asking is our task, even as the Lord encouraged Jeremiah; answering is His responsibility.

Call unto me, and I will answer thee, and show thee great and mighty things, which thou knowest not. Jer. 33:3

Two Ways To Ask Why?

There are questions and then again, there are questions. There are two ways to ask a question. One is acceptable, one unacceptable. A question accompanied by a clenched fist raised towards heaven, is obviously inappropriate. A question accompanied by an inquiring heart seeking understanding of God's will and purposes, I firmly believe, will be both heard and graciously answered.

Recently, I caught a few moments of a science report dealing with creativity on television. The chief researcher said they have discovered after years of study that man is most creative when his mind is not active, when quiet, reflective, meditative or resting. Coincidentally, this same truth is utilized in the next key.

The NIGHT KEY

Wisdom Is Received From God in the Night Season

But there is a God in heaven that revealeth secrets, and maketh known to the king Nebuchadnezzar what shall be in the latter days. Thy dream, and the visions of thy head upon thy bed, are these; As for thee, O king, thy thoughts came into thy mind upon thy bed, what should come to pass hereafter: and he that revealeth secrets maketh known to thee what shall come to pass. Dan. 2:28-29

I saw a dream which made me afraid, and the thoughts upon my bed and the visions of my head troubled me. Dan. 4:5

Thus were the visions of mine head in my bed; I saw... and behold. Dan. 4:10

I saw in the visions of my head upon my bed, and, behold, a watcher and an holy one came down from heaven. Dan. 4:13

But his delight is in the law of the Lord; and in his law doth he meditate day and night. Psa. 1:2

I will bless the Lord, who hath given me counsel: my reins also instruct me in the night seasons. Psa. 16:7

When I remember thee upon my bed, and meditate on thee in the night watches. Psa. 63:6

KEY 2 POSE YOUR QUESTION AT NIGHT

This key, suggested in the preceding verses, is the one which I have personally found to be most valuable.

When Daniel described King Nebuchadnezzar's forgotten dream, he phrased the situation in a question and reiterated that the dream occurred at night.

As for thee, O king, thy thoughts came into thy mind upon thy bed, what should come to pass hereafter: and he that revealeth secrets maketh known to thee what shall come to pass. Dan. 2:29

The king himself had been seeking an answer, at night in his sleep. This principle is so powerful that it apparently applied even to an unbelieving and evil king. The astonished and delighted king exclaimed,

Of a truth it is, that your God is a God of gods, and a Lord of kings, and a revealer of secrets, seeing thou couldest reveal this secret. Dan. 2:47

a great key

Seeking answers in the night, while resting and sleeping, is a recognized brainstorming technique used today. While asleep, when the mind is uncluttered, an individual can function far more creatively. Therefore, pose your question to God *at night.*

The Scriptures repeatedly encourage the reader to mediate upon the Word of God. As a result I try to ask God a question every night, so as not to waste any opportunity to learn from Him. My inquiries are usually as simple as asking what particular passages mean, or how I can help others understand them.

In Job, thought to be the earliest written portion of our Bible, Elihu spoke of hearing from God at night.

For God speaketh once, yea twice, yet man perceiveth it not. In a dream, in a vision of the night, when deep sleep falleth upon men, in slumberings upon the bed; Then he openeth the ears of men, and sealeth their instruction, That he may withdraw man from his purpose, and hide pride from man. Job 33:14-17

Elihu mentions God sealing instruction as a seal is placed on a bottle of oil or wine. When something is put in a vessel, the seal not only keeps it in, but also serves to authenticate what is within. The seal bears the identification of the owner or sealer, in this case the Author-Creator of wisdom and instruction!

God clearly speaks to man while he is asleep, because He must somehow overcome man's natural resistance to change, and to new, previously unperceived truths. He does so through bypassing his resistance while man is sleeping. Man has his own agenda which God seeks to redirect, or *withdraw man from his own purposes.*

In addition to Daniel and Job, David also willfully practiced nightly meditation.

When I remember thee upon my bed, and meditate on thee in the night watches. Psa. 63:6

In Psalm 63 David gave two clues to his seeking God: remembering God, and meditating upon Him in the night.

How precious also are thy thoughts unto me, O God! how great is the sum of them! If I should count them, they are more in number than the sand: when I awake, I am still with thee. Psa. 139:17-18

"When I awake" indicates that the thoughts of God had been accessible to him while asleep.

Another prophet, Samuel, heard from the Lord, and even received His calling, in the night.

And the word of the Lord was precious in those days; there was no open vision...and Samuel was laid down to sleep...the Lord called Samuel...And the Lord called yet again, Samuel...Now Samuel did not yet know the Lord, neither was the word of the Lord yet revealed unto him. And the Lord called Samuel again the third time...And the Lord came, and stood, and called as at other times, Samuel, Samuel. Then Samuel answered, Speak; for thy servant heareth. 1 Sam. 3:1-10

We who are dull of hearing can certainly take heart; Samuel didn't realize until after receiving counsel from another and a fourth summons that it was the Lord speaking to him. This illustrates an occasion when God spoke by grace to a man not expecting to hear. It is comforting to see that God meets us at the level of our understanding and our capacity. A New Testament example illustrates how God accommodates our inadequacies and is willing to restore. (cf. Peter in John 21:15-17)

When asking questions of God utilize the six honest serving men of whom Rudyard Kipling wrote. "I have six honest serving men who serve me *night* and day. They are Who, What, Why, Where, When, and How." [How did they serve him *in the night*? Could Kipling have known something about the power of questions in the night?]

HELPFUL TECHNIQUE -- **Write the Vision**

When hearing from God in the night, it is important to write the revelation lest you lose it, and in order that others might profit from it, as did Daniel our pattern.

Daniel had a dream and visions of his head upon his bed: then he wrote the dream, and told the sum of the matters.
Dan. 7:1

Daniel both wrote and related the dream's message to others, including us. God likewise specifically instructed Habakkuk to "write the vision" granted to him, that others might speedily understand and obey it.

And the Lord...said, Write the vision, and make it plain...that he may run that readeth it Hab. 2:2

HELPFUL TECHNIQUE -- **Keep Recording Materials Handy**

Have materials readily at hand, such as a pencil and paper or a tape recorder, so you can record what the Lord may tell you. He may give me three or four points of revelation about a passage of Scripture that I've prayed to understand. When morning comes, however, I often only recall one or two points unless I have a pen and pad handy. I have learned that I'm usually too lazy to get up and get paper and pen in the dark; it is too easy to convince myself that I'll surely remember something so perfect. I may not, and often even the very arrangement of the wording is significant.

What is the last thing on your mind at night? A television program? Take time to settle your mind to reflect upon God before retiring. In today's world of media stimulation this truly takes self-discipline.

One additional benefit of this habit is the controlling of one's thoughts at night. Many people have complained of having difficulty in controlling their thought life while in bed at night. Therefore, pray the Scriptures; meditate upon the Scriptures. This is accomplished by reviewing a parable. Put yourself in it and ask Him to explain it to you, as the Psalmist said,

Sin not: commune with your own heart upon your bed, and be still. Psa. 4:4

Wisdom Also Often Comes Early in the Morning

O God, thou art my God; early will I seek thee: my soul thirsteth for thee, my flesh longeth for thee Psa. 63:1

And I spake unto you, rising up early and speaking...and I called you Jer. 7:13

Hearken to the words of my servants the prophets, whom I sent unto you, both rising up early, and sending them Jer. 26:5

The Lord God hath given me the tongue of the learned, that I should know how to speak a word in season to him that is weary: he wakeneth morning by morning, he wakeneth mine ear to hear as the learned. Isa. 50:4

I love them that love me; and those that seek me early shall find me. Prov. 8:17

A natural corollary to gaining wisdom at night is seeking Him in the morning before the day begins. He also desires for us to seek Him early in the morning.

Often a question forms in the mind early in the morning, during the best daytime seeking time, while our minds are fresh and we are alert. Yet frequently, we must await the answers which often come at night, as they did for Daniel.

In the daytime one's mind quickly becomes preoccupied with the activities of the day. There are many demands upon our daytime hours. However, the night times are times of relinquishment to rest. There seem to be two corollary aspects in receiving from God: dedicating both beginnings and endings, mornings and evenings, to the Lord.

Famine Of Hearing

Behold, the days come, saith the Lord God, that I will send a famine in the land, not a famine of bread, nor a thirst for water, but of hearing the words of the Lord. Amos 8:11

In our day there is no famine in the availability of the Word of God, Christian materials or Bibles. There are more Bibles in this country today, than have previously existed since Scriptures were first recorded, and yet there is still a dearth, a famine of the hearing of the Word of God.

We must learn to hear from God continuously, not just once or twice, or occasionally, but daily. There is a need each morning for fresh manna. "Give us this day our daily bread," especially, if it has not been delivered to us during the night. The Israelites had to gather each morning to their fresh manna for that day. The manna that was not gathered and used right away could not be utilized later because *...it bred worms, and stank.* The manna had to be obtained when available and used that same day, or it was lost forever.

Fresh revelation from the Lord is similar. God cannot give me a word of guidance for today, tomorrow! I must seek Him this morning for today, because today's missed guidance if received tomorrow would only bring condemnation.

Hunger Is A Qualification

Blessed are they which do hunger and thirst after righteousness: for they shall be filled. Mat. 5:6

He hath filled the hungry with good things. Luke 1:53a

If in the natural your appetite is satisfied, you will cease to hunger and will not keep on eating natural food. So it is with the supernatural and spiritual food. If we cease to hunger spiritually, we will cease seeking God for revelation.

For example, the hungry lion goes out hunting food, but when he is full he is content to remain in his den or sleep in the sun. Hunger drives the lion to its next meal, and in the same fashion hunger for spiritual truth drives us toward our next revelation. Once you have tasted the fresh manna of new revelation from God, I guarantee that you will want to feast again.

Every morning we can begin our day gathering what God has provided for us, by recapping or recording the revelations granted during the night, and partaking of his mercies (and fresh revelations) which are new each morning.

It is...the Lord's mercies...his compassions...They are new every morning: great is thy faithfulness. Lam. 3:22-23

Keep your bread fresh; don't let anyone or anything divert your hunger for God. Seek and hunger for God Himself. Cultivate and nurture your own sincere hunger for God alone. Do not allow it to be stifled by the cares of the world, fatigue, pride, laziness, or religion.

God's ability comes to those whom the Holy Ghost has touched, has prepared, who are seeking all God has for them, and who are *open* to everything God has for them.

Many times the question pondered and meditated upon during the night pops gently to mind in the morning. When God awakens the believer's hearing, his ability to hear the answer, which He has been trying to communicate, often comes without further effort.

There is something special about early morning time with the Lord. Our minds are usually fresher, clear and uncluttered by the problems of the day which we have not yet encountered. Thus, we are more attentive, and sensitive to the Lord.

I prevented the dawning of the morning, and cried: I hoped in thy word. Psa. 119:147

This may be rendered literally, "I am up before dawn to hear thy promises." God has in fact promised to be found of us when we seek Him early.

I love them that love me; and those that seek me early shall find me. Prov. 8:17

The WHOLEHEARTED KEY

Wisdom comes to the wholehearted seeker of God

Blessed are they that keep his testimonies, and that seek him with the whole heart. Psa. 119:2

But if...thou shalt seek the Lord thy God, thou shalt find him, if thou seek him with all thy heart and with all thy soul. Deut. 4:29

Now set your heart and your soul to seek the Lord your God. 1 Chr. 22:19a

And they entered into a covenant to seek the Lord God of their fathers with all their heart and with all their soul. 2 Chr. 15:12

And I set my face unto the Lord God, to seek by prayer and supplications, with fasting, and sackcloth, and ashes. Dan. 9:3

KEY 3 **SEEK HIM WITH YOUR WHOLE HEART**

God has promised to be found by us when we seek Him with wholehearted abandonment.

And thou shalt love the Lord thy God with all thy heart, and with all thy soul, and with all thy mind, and with all thy strength: this is the first commandment. Mark 12:30

Focus; Determination; Fasting

And I set my face unto the Lord God, to seek by prayer and supplications, with fasting, and sackcloth, and ashes.
Dan. 9:3

Another aspect of Daniel's seeking God was determination. He was committed to getting an answer. He *set his face* to seek the Lord by prayer, supplication, fasting, and sackcloth and ashes. Each of these is a different category. Supplication is asking, beseeching, seeking mercy; fasting is a form of humbling himself; and the extreme form of humbling is in sackcloth and ashes.

In the twenty-fourth chapter of Luke there is a beautiful confirmation of the principle that God blesses those who make a sincere effort to understand His Word and working. While two disciples were on the road to Emmaus communing and reasoning among themselves, their answer arrived in the form of the Risen Lord Himself, who came to them in an unrecognized form, to provide the answer which they sought!

And it came to pass, that, while they communed together and reasoned, Jesus himself drew near, and went with them. Ought not Christ to have suffered these things, and to enter into his glory? And beginning at Moses and all the prophets, he expounded unto them in all the scriptures the things concerning himself. Luk. 24:26-27

Jesus explained the Scriptures to them bringing various Scriptures to bear upon the very question which they posed. He used the Word to explain it to them. He was The Word of God, the *Logos*, explaining Himself, the *Logos*, to them! He also confirmed our premise, that all the Scriptures contain truths concerning Jesus.

Afterwards as the two reflected upon their experience their reactions were similar to those of each of us, who have similarly been blessed with discovering new depths of meaning in the Scriptures,

Did not our heart burn within us, while he talked with us by the way, and while he opened to us the scriptures?
Luke 24:32

Delight thyself also in the Lord; and he shall give thee the desires of thine heart. Psa. 37:4

In His Word God has promised to grant the desires of our hearts. Also remember, God has no grandsons, only sons. Every believer is equally eligible for the blessing of finding God's truths, if he will diligently apply himself to the task.

God Grants Wisdom to Those Who Practice Repentance, Obedience, Holiness, and Righteousness.

Whom shall he teach knowledge? and whom shall he make to understand doctrine? them that are weaned from the milk, and drawn from the breasts. Isa. 28:9

For every one that useth milk is unskilful in the word of righteousness: for he is a babe. But strong meat belongeth to them that are of full age, even those who by reason of use have their senses exercised to discern both good and evil. Heb. 5:13-14

Abiding is still another qualification.
If ye abide in me, and my words abide in you, ye shall ask what ye will, and it shall be done unto you. John 15:7

KEY 4 **GOD REQUIRES ROHR**

Repentance,
Obedience,
Holiness, and
Righteousness.

In order to attain and remain righteous we must repent, obey, and seek to be holy. Since Jesus is our righteousness, we must submit to Him, accept Him in all His fullness and obey Him fully, which includes accepting as our Teacher, His Successor, the Holy Spirit, He promised to send.

Repentance Is a Key

As it is written in the law of Moses, all this evil is come upon us: yet made we not our prayer before the Lord our God, that we might turn from our iniquities, and understand thy truth. Dan. 9:13

Repentance is a key to understanding God's truth. We should regularly make it our prayer that we turn from our iniquities and *understand thy truth.* If you expect to meaningfully hear from God, you must willfully turn from all your known iniquities.

This is simply common sense to the New Testament Christian; he knows from Scripture that he is cleansed from sin and thus able to approach God's throne in faith, with a clear conscience.

But if we walk in the light, as he is in the light, we have fellowship one with another, and the blood of Jesus Christ his Son cleanseth us from all sin. 1 John 1:7

Let us draw near with a true heart in full assurance of faith, having our hearts sprinkled from an evil conscience, and our bodies washed with pure water. Heb. 10:22

God has promised,
Turn you at my reproof: behold, I will pour out my spirit unto you, I will make known my words unto you.
Prov. 1:23

Obedience Is a Key

Jesus warned His hearers in Mark 4:24, *Take heed what ye hear*, and again in Luke 8:18, *Take heed therefore how ye hear.* The "what" will determine the "how," if we truly recognize that it is the very voice of God which we hear in the Word of God, we will listen differently than if we were merely hearing man's words or man's wisdom. We need to hear His words with reverence and awe, and must seek to obey them fully. Those who have come under the influence of modern theology, higher criticism, or any of the other forms of teaching which diminish or deny the inspiration of Scripture, have introduced a cancer into their hope of faith.

If ye be willing and obedient, ye shall eat the good of the land: Isa. 1:19

In all thy ways acknowledge him, and he shall direct thy paths. Prov. 3:6

Samuel knew the importance which God attached to obedience.

Hath the Lord as great delight in burnt offerings and sacrifices, as in obeying the voice of the Lord? Behold, to obey is better than sacrifice, and to hearken than the fat of rams. 1 Sam 15:22

As we submit to (obey) Him in all our ways, He will give us the direction which we require. The Apostle Paul testified,

I was not disobedient unto the heavenly vision.

Acts 26:19

Like Paul, be obedient. Be obedient to the Word of God and to any "heavenly vision" which God may choose to grant to you.

Logically, one would not expect God to continue speaking to someone who does not obey what He is being told. Why should God bother speaking to us, revealing concepts, or giving instruction, if we aren't doing what He has previously told us to do? We must be willing both to receive and *to obey* what He reveals to us.

This is an important key. A common phrase today is "use it or lose it." This is true in the natural world; if one does not use muscles, they atrophy. The same principle is relevant to spiritual issues also; if we do not heed the gentle voice and leadings of the Spirit of God, He will soon cease to speak to us.

Don't expect God to give you another revelation if you haven't yet obeyed the last one. Obedience keeps revelations coming. Obedience is somewhat like priming a pump, to start the water flowing.

This may be expressed as a formula:

Knowledge of God =
(love of God) + (obedience to God)

Obedience may also be expressed as a formula:

Obedience = **(hearing) + (obeying)**

Hear and Obey

The sheep who belong to the Good Shepherd hear His voice. He places spiritual brands upon the ears and upon the feet of His sheep. *My sheep,* He said, *hear my voice* and *they follow me.* Those sheep hear and obey Him; those who are not His sheep do not hear, and therefore do not follow, but go astray instead.

To truly hear Him is to know Him, although it is also true, that to know Him is to hear Him.

And when he putteth forth his own sheep, he goeth before them, and the sheep follow him: for they know his voice.
John 10:4

Holiness Is a Key

God has called us to perfection, or maturity.

Be ye therefore perfect, even as your Father which is in heaven is perfect. Mat. 5:48

Be ye holy; for I am holy. 1 Pet. 1:16

One of the ministries of the Spirit of Holiness, another name for the Holy Spirit, is to make us holy, as God has promised:

And I will put my spirit within you, and cause you to walk in my statutes, and ye shall keep my judgments, and do them. Ezek. 36:27

Righteousness Is a Key

But seek ye first the kingdom of God, and his righteousness; and all these things shall be added unto you.
Mat. 6:33

As we seek the Kingdom of God first (the central figure of the kingdom is its King, who also is the *Righteousness* of God) He can give us all the other things we may desire, among which are wisdom and understanding. God manifested Himself in the flesh, in Christ, who is the Sun of Righteousness. Righteousness is a qualification for successful praying and for obtaining answers from God.

The effectual fervent prayer of a righteous man availeth much. James 5:16b

Wisdom Comes Through Interpretation

Declaring the end from the beginning, and from ancient times the things that are not yet done, saying, My counsel shall stand, and I will do all my pleasure. Isaiah 46:10

So shall my word be that goeth forth out of my mouth: it shall not return unto me void, but it shall accomplish that which I please, and it shall prosper in the thing whereto I sent it. Isaiah 55:11

But we speak the wisdom of God in a mystery, even the hidden wisdom, which God ordained before the world unto our glory: 1 Cor. 2:7

But as it is written, eye hath not seen, nor ear heard, neither have entered into the heart of man, the things which God hath prepared for them that love him. But God hath revealed them unto us by his Spirit: for the Spirit searcheth all things, yea, the deep things of God. 1 Cor. 2:9-10

For my thoughts are not your thoughts, neither are your ways my ways, saith the Lord. For as the heavens are higher than the earth, so are my ways higher than your ways, and my thoughts than your thoughts. Isaiah 55:9

KEY 5 **SUBMIT FULLY TO THE TEACHER.**

The answer to every question may be found in the Word of God (the *Logos*), but it may be encoded in symbolism. Thus, one needs the aid of the Interpreter, the Revealer, the Teacher, the Holy Spirit.

When we present a question to God, we acknowledge our ignorance; our inability to find the answers on our own. So then, in effect, we call upon, rely upon, the Holy Spirit to assist in our praying. Even though we don't know how to pray correctly, our spirit cries out to God for help.

Likewise the Spirit also helpeth our infirmities: for we know not what we should pray for as we ought: but the Spirit itself maketh intercession for us with groanings which cannot be uttered. Rom. 8:26

The Holy Spirit will intercede for us with a sigh, a groan, an inexpressible, wordless cry, too deep to utter in articulate speech, as He carries our requests to the Throne. The believer needs to receive the Holy Spirit in all His fullness, and all of Him that he can obtain. Do not settle for less than God's best. Do not settle for the status quo, or for any theological limitations, which tend to make His clear promises of no effect as Jesus warned,

Making the word of God of none effect through your tradition. Mark 7:13

The Holy Spirit Enables Us to Hear

And the spirit entered into me when he spake unto me, and set me upon my feet, that I heard him that spake unto me. Ezek. 2:2

The Holy Spirit is a code-breaker whose stated ministry is to reveal those things which God has chosen to conceal from the understanding of the natural man, but to grant understanding to His own.

But the natural man receiveth not the things of the Spirit of God: for they are foolishness unto him: neither can he know them, because they are spiritually discerned.

1 Cor. 2:14

But we speak the wisdom of God in a mystery, even the hidden wisdom, which God ordained before the world unto our glory: But as it is written, eye hath not seen, nor ear heard, neither have entered into the heart of man, the things which God hath prepared for them that love him. But God hath revealed them unto us by his Spirit: for the Spirit searcheth all things, yea, the deep things of God.

1 Cor. 2:7,9-10

Now we have received, not the spirit of the world, but the spirit which is of God; that we might know the things that are freely given to us of God. 1 Cor. 2:12

These Scriptures describe the function of the Holy Spirit's ministry. Without the Holy Spirit's help it is as if we were standing at the door of an unlighted treasure-filled vault equipped with only a flickering torch. The Holy Spirit's ministry is to enlighten us, to bring illumination to bear upon the contents; that we might see and know the riches which God has in store for us. God desires for His people to see and fully understand what He has provided, as Paul prayed:

That the God of our Lord Jesus Christ, the Father of glory, may give unto you the spirit of wisdom and revelation in the knowledge of him: The eyes of your understanding being enlightened; that ye may know what is the hope of his calling, and what the riches of the glory of his inheritance in the saints. Eph. 1:17-18

Our inheritance is now because Christ has died. No inheritance can be given until the testator, the maker of the will, dies. Regrettably, we are ignorant of our inheritance and the Holy Spirit must show us what has already been granted to us.

The Holy Spirit "comes alongside to help in time of need" and illuminates the room with His light. He does not create more for you to see, but merely illuminates what God has already provided for you in your inheritance.

Many believers have missed much of what God intended for them, because they have either restricted, or not embraced fully the ministry of the Holy Spirit. God has many treasures to reveal, but they are only seen by those supernaturally and spiritually equipped to receive such revelation. These are things that must be revealed by the Holy Spirit; by God's design He is the Revealer!

Just one experience when His Holy Spirit reveals truth is worth a previous lifetime of struggling to know on our own. Jesus sent Him as our Teacher.

But the Comforter, which is the Holy Ghost, whom the Father will send in my name, he shall teach you all things, and bring all things to your remembrance, whatsoever I have said unto you. John 14:26

Progressive, Ongoing Revelation

Even when Jesus was here in the flesh, while the Perfect was present, mankind in general and His disciples in particular, could not bear to hear all that He had to tell them.

I have yet many things to say unto you, but ye cannot bear them now. John 16:12

They were not yet ready to receive, nor prepared to learn all that He knew they needed to know. His clear implication is that they will learn those truths later, under the tutelage of another Teacher.

These things have I spoken unto you, being yet present with you. But the Comforter, which is the Holy Ghost, whom the Father will send in my name, he shall teach you all things. John 14:25-26

[The Comforter] *...will guide you into all truth...and will show you things to come.* John 16:13

What was true for those disciples, is true for us as well: we, too, are not yet ready to receive all that he has for us, that is why He lovingly gives us bit by bit, line upon line.

When...the Spirit of truth, is come, he will guide you into all truth. John 16:13

Who among us can claim to possess all truth, to know all things, or fully grasp all that Jesus intended in the words which He spoke? This is something yet to be attained. Yet the Holy Spirit has been promised to do just that for us by the Logos, the very Word of God, Himself. What a promise. What a challenge, to know all things!

Prophecy or revelation begins in God; it is a message revealed to, or spoken through, a person usually coming in an encoded fashion. Yet, it is revealed, and therefore necessitates an interpretation, because it may come in the form of a dream, a vision, or as words little understood.

The Holy Spirit today still may communicate via dreams, revelations or visions and therefore, from the same Spirit must come the interpretation, or the illumination of understanding, if the message contained within is to be understood.

Wisdom Is Acquired Through Study.

The heart of the righteous studieth to answer.
Prov. 15:28a

And that ye study to be quiet, and to do your own business.
1 Thes. 4:11

Study to show thyself approved unto God, a workman that needeth not to be ashamed, rightly dividing the word of truth.
2 Tim. 2:15

And keep the charge of the Lord thy God, to walk in his ways, to keep his statutes, and his commandments, and his judgments, and his testimonies, as it is written in the law of Moses, that thou mayest prosper in all that thou doest.
1 Kings. 2:3

And the king...made a covenant before the Lord, to walk after the Lord, and to keep his commandments and his testimonies and his statutes with all their heart and all their soul, to perform the words of this covenant that were written in this book. And all the people stood to the covenant.
2 Kings 23:3

KEY 6

APPLY YOURSELF; BECOME A STUDENT

In the first year of his reign I Daniel understood by books the number of the years, whereof the word of the Lord came to Jeremiah the prophet, that he would accomplish seventy years in the desolations of Jerusalem. Dan. 9:2

Daniel studied books in addition to the Scriptures to enhance his understanding. Paul endorsed this principle in the New Testament.

Study to show thyself approved unto God, a workman that needeth not to be ashamed, rightly dividing the word of truth. 2 Tim. 2:15

Paul did not recommend a return to the Tree of Knowledge, but rather a seeking of Godly wisdom through study of the Word of God. The Bible first and foremost, but wisdom and accumulated knowledge are available in the writings of anointed men of God.

David is another witness to this truth. He made the same observation that understanding comes from study of the Word.

All this, said David, the Lord made me understand in writing by his hand upon me, even all the works of this pattern. 1 Chr. 28:19

It is equally clear that God works according to His purposes or plans, and He loves for man to discover and to understand the patterns, symbolic purposes, and plans which He employs. I believe that God, like any master architect or artist, loves to reveal and explain His works to those who love Him.

God also answers questions and reveals His will through circumstances. Hundreds of times when I have been trying to understand something either in the Word of God, or in the supernatural realm, God has given me the answer parenthetically through something I read in an entirely unrelated area. Most frequently, however, it was while studying in the Word, seeking an answer to a different question that I have discovered the answer to the earlier question which I had placed on a back burner.

This accidental discovery of truth is similar to something I have often observed in my own ministry of teaching from the Bible over the past twenty-five years. It is truly exciting to teach under the anointing of the Holy Spirit; on dozens of occasions, I have had people come to me after a meeting when I had taught on witnessing, and thank me for answering all their questions on *tithing*!

The first few times this occurred I was dumbfounded, because, as in this case, I had not mentioned tithe or tithing. Somehow the Lord was answering their questions, and teaching them what they wanted to know. It is very humbling to learn that God was teaching something through me of which I was unaware.

God and his truth always meet us on the basis of a promise. Find a promise for your situation in the Word of God.

HELPFUL TECHNIQUE -- **Aids to Study**

Just as Daniel studied books, so we can take advantage of study aids. I have found it very helpful to use Hebrew-English, Greek-English dictionaries such as *Strong's*

Exhaustive Concordance to find exact or alternative renderings of words in the Scripture. A regular English Dictionary is another surprisingly simple but effective tool. It is surprising what may sometimes be learned by the exact meaning of a word, or the alternative meanings of the word. Many years ago my wife had a dream about a python one night during a struggle with anxiety. She was led to look up the meaning of python in the dictionary and discovered as an alternative rendering, "pythoness" which meant "fortune-teller." As a result she renounced her pre-salvation involvement with fortune-tellers and was set free from anxiety.

Do your part by reading and studying the Scriptures. God may want to speak to you through His written Word. Read other writings on the subject; read if you can what He has already given to others on the subject you are researching. There is no need to reinvent the wheel; if God has already given the answer to someone else, He doesn't need to do it over again. He can and might do so for you, but read and study to learn what He has already revealed.

It is important to apply ourselves to seriously seeking God, because the riches of the Word are often, just below the surface, just beyond the grasp of the lazy, or those unwilling to do a little "digging." To obtain the greatest riches of God's Word, like a natural prospector we are usually required to do some digging (studying).

I heard a powerful prophetic vision more than twenty years ago. A prophet shared that while he was driving across Oklahoma, the Lord spoke to him and showed him in the Spirit, that there were great riches (oil) available just beneath the surface, but, the Lord said, "Most men will not bother to dig to find it. The greater part of the few who did seek, quit drilling too soon." Much of the land in Oklahoma was considered to be too dry and thus was not valued. As a result much of it was given to the Indians.

Even though man missed it, because of his unwillingness to persevere in searching, nevertheless *the great riches were still there.*

Finally, **don't expect God to give something already given!** If He has already stated His will, you don't need a revelation on the subject. As I told a minister from another state who came to our prayer room for help a few years ago, "You don't need a special revelation or an audible word from heaven to know that incest and adultery are wrong. God has plainly told you so in His word. That voice telling you, 'It's okay in your case, is a delusion!'"

The MEDIATATION KEY

Wisdom Comes Through Meditation.

This book of the law shall not depart out of thy mouth; but thou shalt meditate therein day and night, that thou mayest observe to do according to all that is written therein: for then thou shalt make thy way prosperous, and then thou shalt have good success. Josh. 1:8

And these words, which I command thee this day, shall be in thine heart: And thou shalt teach them diligently unto thy children, and shalt talk of them when thou sittest in thine house, and when thou walkest by the way, and when thou liest down, and when thou risest up. Deut. 6:6-7

I will meditate also of all thy work, and talk of thy doings. Psa. 77:12

I will meditate in thy precepts, and have respect unto thy ways. Psa. 119:15

Thy servant did meditate in thy statutes. Psa. 119:23

I remember the days of old; I meditate on all thy works; I muse on the work of thy hands. Psa. 143:5

Meditate upon these things; give thyself wholly to them; that thy profiting may appear to all. 1 Tim. 4:15

KEY 7 **MEDITATE CREATIVELY.**

Be creative in your approach to the Scriptures. In the preceding Scriptures the recurring theme is seen of meditation during the day and night. There is great reward in seeking God in the night.

What is meditation? It is defined in the Hebrew as "to ponder, to muse, to talk with oneself (about)"; in the Greek, "to revolve in the mind." Mediation for the Christian differs from a fixation upon self, practiced by the world. It is a focusing upon God, and upon His words, deeds, and teaching, a contemplation or reflection upon His holy Word

How to Meditate Creatively

If you have a question, about a passage of Scripture, prayerfully ask God to give you understanding. Keep reading and meditating upon that passage; personalize it, attempt to put yourself into the situation, try to mentally live it, all the while allowing God to turn the account around in your mind, to show you possible variations of what might have occurred. Ponder it, muse about it, talk with yourself about it.

Seek To Actually Experience the Scripture

In the night time, meditate upon your bed. Mentally put yourself in the situation. As you meditate upon the passage of Scripture, imagine yourself in each of the roles: as a disciple hearing Jesus' teaching; as each character either in the parable He is relating, or in the action described. Try to think what you would feel if you were the returning prodigal son, as the elder brother, or as the expectant, and then joyful father.

You will gain fresh appreciation for each of the passages which you personally experience in this way. In addition, you will gain insights and understanding as you employ this method.

A Key can look foolish to others. Thus far the methods which have been presented for seeking God's wisdom have seemed pretty rational and socially acceptable, but there are some "faith" things which do not make any sense to our natural minds. The following method is for those who are desperate enough to be willing to be a fool for Christ in order to obtain His wisdom.

Yea, if thou criest after knowledge, and liftest up thy voice for understanding. Prov. 2:3

Are you prepared to cry out to God, not figuratively but literally? Lift up your voice aloud to obtain knowledge and understanding. I suggest that if you decide to use this technique of desperation, that you make sure you are alone.

Doth not wisdom cry? and understanding put forth her voice? Prov. 8:1

Wisdom crieth without; she uttereth her voice in the streets. Prov. 1:20

When all else fails, and you are truly desperate, cry out to God!

We need to provide the other half of the equation; as Daniel had to persevere on the earthly side, while Michael and his reinforcements were battling through from Heaven's side. Wisdom and understanding speak, but who will listen? Wisdom is doing her part and crying out to us from the heavenly side of the equation. Apparently if we will do our part, and cry out, wisdom and understanding will also respond in kind.

Expect opposition if you diligently seek the Lord in the word. Overcoming is a qualification for receiving. The one who will hear from God must overcome distractions that are designed to prevent the hearing of His voice. Overcome the enemy's opposition, because Satan hates overcomers and those men who will choose to diligently seek God. Therefore, seek Him earnestly.

Hear what the Spirit saith...To him that overcometh will I give to eat of the hidden manna. Rev. 2:17

Also expect opposition to your growing in the Lord, to seeking God for knowledge, wisdom, understanding, or guidance. Beware of any cares or carelessness, sorrows or pleasure, poverty or wealth, anything, that could fill your heart, to the exclusion of the will and Word of God.

I have learned in nearly twenty-five years of ministry, that the greater the opposition, the greater the blessings that will follow. The more opposition Satan throws in your path, the bigger the impact God has planned for your obedience. I have found that the more difficulty encountered in delivering something (giving a convicting message, physically getting to a place to pray for someone), the greater the healing or blessing intended.[6] The degree of opposition is proportional to the importance which God attaches to your activity.

[6] A dramatic example of this is the case of LeRoy related in the book *Three Kinds of Faith*.

Satan seems to sense the importance God attaches to certain events. It may be, as some have suggested that although Satan cannot read God's mind, he and his forces can detect increased angelic activity directed toward the area of your request, and so he corresponds with additional forces to attempt to frustrate God's intentions to bless or use you! He will also attempt to block your drawing nigh to God in prayer, in Bible study, and in fellowship.

Counterfeiting is an even more subtle form of opposition. The Enemy has done an excellent job of frightening believers away from several areas of God's truth simply because he has staked an occult claim to the same territory. He has established counterfeit and pseudo-sciences which cause believers to withdraw, fearing any contact. Satan has promoted astrology as a means of fortune-telling and as a result, many Christians are even afraid of valid astronomy and fearful of anything to do with the constellations. Because of this fear, many Christians miss the knowledge contained in the constellations which God created, numbered and named, as He did all the stars. (Psa. 147:4, Isa. 40:26; 45:12)

Satan has also promoted numerology, thus many Christians fear gematria, the study of the numerical value of the letters in the Hebrew and Greek alphabets, which have surprising messages for believers (See chapter six). God has written His word not only in words but has also included his numerical signature and or coded messages in the numerical value of the letters of the text.

I encountered an extreme example of how the phenomenon of legalism and fear can affect people in our Christian bookstore a few years ago. An elderly woman began berating me for carrying a line of rainbow decals among the stickers in our store. I politely and silently endured her abuse for a while, but then I began to sense a holy and righteous anger arising within me. I recalled that Paul spoke of others also in the bondage of legalism.

To whom we gave place by subjection, no, not for an hour; that the truth of the gospel might continue with you.
Gal. 2:5

Consequently, I attempted to answer her in love. She kept interrupting me until finally I said, "Wait just a minute, Ma'am. Let's get things straight. Simply because Satan has claimed the rainbow as an occult symbol, doesn't make it an occult symbol, nor does it give him ownership! Who created the Rainbow? Remember, God said, *I do set my bow in the cloud, and it shall be for a token of a covenant between me and the earth*." Gen. 9:13

God said it was *His bow* that He gave as a sign of *His covenant* with man. Satan would love to have us avoid or forget any reminders of God's covenants.

Although the elderly woman's daughter kept nodding vigorous assent to each of my statements, and said several times "He's totally right, Mom," the elderly woman left still muttering under her breath about my having 'sold out to Satan.'

Jesus, Himself, cautioned God's people not to be gullible, or deceived.

The next chapter contains encouragement and helpful techniques for seeking answers from God.

CHAPTER FIVE

PRACTICAL HELPS AND ENCOURAGEMENTS

Some spiritual qualifications facilitate successfully seeking and receiving truth from God, in addition to those mentioned in KEY 4, ROHR.

1.) You need to **Be** properly related to God. You must have accepted His offer of adoption back into His family, i.e., **Be** His child.)

2.) Your motivation must **Be** righteous

3.) You need the Teacher; **Be** open to the Holy Spirit, who is the now present member of the Godhead sent as Teacher, the office formerly occupied by Jesus. When Jesus was on earth, He was the designated representative of the Godhead, appointed as the revealer of hidden truths. Since Jesus won the right to pour forth the Spirit by His completed work, and did so at Pentecost, that task now belongs to the Holy Spirit.

The four Be's above are capitalized and in boldfaced type. That was done to emphasize and introduce the following section which consists of twenty-one Be's, things we should either be, or be doing, if we are to "be" successful in tapping into God's wisdom.

A SERIES OF TWENTY-ONE BE S

BE Available to Receive

When awaiting an important long distance phone call from a loved one, you will make it a point to remain near the phone. You will make yourself available to receive the call. Make yourself available to God, by setting aside time with Him, and by actively seeking Him.

BE a Seeker of Answers

But seek ye first the kingdom of God, and his righteousness; and all these things shall be added unto you.

Mat. 6:33

In my youth, I was a seeker of riches, literally a prospector, for gold and more especially searching for rubies and sapphires with slight success. Today, I prize a glimmer of inspiration far more than I formerly did the glitter of gold in a prospecting pan and have the joy of seeking souls, jewels for God's crown.

BE Still Before God

Be still, and know that I am God...I will be exalted in the earth. Psa. 46:10

Be still when God commands, "Be still!" He's being polite. What He really means is "Shut up!" We are usually so busy telling Him what to do, and how to do it, that we don't listen nearly enough.

Many years ago while conducting a healing service, I found myself attempting to minister to a group of Pentecostal people who were praying so loudly that I could barely even hear myself. No one was being healed, and it seemed a scene of utter confusion, with everyone praying for himself in his own way. I realized there was no possible way for them to *be in one accord*, or even to *pray in agreement* with me, because they couldn't hear me. So I quickly prayed for wisdom and especially for a way to help these dear people receive. He instantly placed in my mind the analogy of a CB Radio, so I simply told them:

"The Lord just showed me a CB Radio as a key to help you receive healing. You know how a CB radio operates: you push down on the microphone button to transmit, and let the button up to receive. You cannot receive any incoming messages on your CB so long as you are transmitting. You have to stop transmitting and release the mike control in order to receive incoming transmissions."

"I believe that the Lord has just shown me that praying for healing works in a very similar way. So long as we are trying to tell Him what we need, what to do, or how to do it, He can't transmit, and we cannot receive! We need to do what He commanded when He told us to, *Be still, and know that I am God.* (Psa. 46:10) For Him to be exalted, in this case as Healer, we must cease from our own efforts, rest and trust in Him, (be still) and allow Him the freedom to act."

Most believers are busy telling God what needs to be done. I suspect that much prayer for healing and for other needs is somewhat insulting to God. Much praying seems to treat Him as if He weren't quite as intelligent as we are, and therefore the one praying goes into great detail to explain all the symptoms to Him so that He can understand the problem and won't make a mistake.

Too many prayers sound something like this: "Dear God, please do points 1, 2, and 3, for poor little Johnny Smith who has a bad liver, a low blood count, and the doctors don't think he will live."

Recognize the fact that God already knows more about Johnny Smith and his liver than you, or the doctors, will ever know. God knows everything!

We must learn to follow His admonition to be still, because,

The words of the wise are heard in quiet. Eccl. 9:17a

We need to be quiet before Him, listening for the sound of His voice and for His gentle nudging upon our hearts. Keep in mind that so long as you are transmitting, you cannot receive: take time to listen to God. I am speaking to myself as well, for I, too, need to spend more time listening.

HELPFUL TECHNIQUE -- **Create A Quiet Zone**

Most of us are so accustomed to our noisy world, that we may not feel comfortable without some background noise playing, such as cassettes, radio or television. You may find it necessary to enforce a quiet zone. The enforcing will relate probably only to yourself. I find that one way to get some quiet time is to shut off the radio in my car, to shut off the television when home alone. I feel God will not compete with the noise I have chosen. I must shut off the noise if I am to hear His gentle, still, small voice. I must choose to offer Him the heart of a willing, listening servant.

BE Expecting

The main reason most believers don't hear from God, as I have suggested, is because they don't listen. They aren't expecting Him to speak, and thus aren't listening or attuned to Him. So we must decide to listen, and focus our attention and hearing toward Him. To "listen expectantly" means with faith; for we should be expecting Him to speak to us! We might restate this as, be expecting to hear from God; anticipate an answer.

BE Attuned to God

In order to hear God, one must be listening. You may recall a popular Gospel song a few years ago, "Turn Your Radio On." The concept of that song speaks to the issue at hand: one cannot receive the message, or even hear the station, if the radio isn't both turned on, and tuned in. We have to choose to listen to the right station. Unfortunately, many have turned off their receivers for a variety of reasons.

Last year a woman, whom I knew to have been previously blessed with a great prophetic gift, came to one of the sessions I was teaching on this subject. I recognized the woman and remembered how mightily and consistently she had been used nearly twenty years earlier. Realizing that she was not moving in her gift, I asked if she'd let us pray for her. She did. Afterward, we learned that she had turned the gift off because of rejection experienced from churches which had refused to accept her gift of prophecy. The following week she returned and spoke a beautifully anointed prophetic word at our meeting.

BE Renewed to Receive

In order to get good reception, the receiver must be turned on, functioning properly, and be tuned to the proper channel. When a man is saved he obtains a receiver, in the form of a renewed mind:

And be not conformed to this world: but be ye transformed by the renewing of your mind, that ye may prove what is that good, and acceptable, and perfect, will of God.
Rom. 12:2

Only a renewed mind can receive God's knowledge.

But the natural man receiveth not the things of the Spirit of God: for they are foolishness unto him: neither can he know them, because they are spiritually discerned.
1 Cor. 2:14

When a believer has a quickened spirit, a renewed mind, he recognizes his lack of God's presence and seeks to learn more about the loving Father from whom he has so long been estranged, as in the prodigal son.

Be ye not as the horse, or as the mule, which have no understanding. Psa. 32:9

BE Determined

Daniel was a man of great desires, who set both his face, and his heart to know of God, the things he needed or desired to know! He was a wholehearted seeker.

BE Patient

Don't be in too big a hurry. Be patient like Daniel at the river Chebar in Daniel, chapter ten. He waited twenty-one days for his answer to come.

The mother of a woman from our little fellowship came to see me rejoicing, "I've just got to tell you. My husband has finally accepted Jesus. I have been praying for his salvation for 40 years!"

I was both awed, and humbled by her faith. I suspect if I hadn't had my prayer answered within a few months or years, I'd have given up. But praise be to God, she didn't! She is a modern example of perseverance.

I can safely promise that you will be amazed at what God will teach you as you learn to wait patiently upon Him.

Rest in the Lord, and wait patiently for him. Psa. 37:7

Like this woman and Daniel be willing to await the answer. Some things take time; sometimes God's answers are delayed en route, as in Daniel, chapter ten.

BE Open to Hear

Decide you will hear from whatever source God may choose to use, and whomever God may choose to use. I must confess to falling prey to this common block. I would like to help you avoid my mistakes.

The first time I ever heard a prophecy, the prophet used a double negative. He included "don't" two times in a sentence where neither belonged. I mentally concluded, "That cannot be God speaking, because my God would speak perfect English."

Later I learned two important lessons: that God isn't squeamish, but uses yielded willing vessels who may not always be perfectly educated; and that it is the message and not the messenger that is of the utmost importance.

But the prophet, which shall presume to speak a word in my name, which I have not commanded him to speak, or that shall speak in the name of other gods, even that prophet shall die. Deut. 18:20

Although the evaluation of prophecies is of utmost importance, prophecies can be valid without specifically referring to you. They sometimes have a time frame; and the classic tests for prophecy must now be tempered with loving New Testament judgment, assessment or evaluation.

Let the prophets speak two or three, and let the other judge. If any thing be revealed to another that sitteth by, let the first hold his peace. For ye may all prophesy one by one, that all may learn, and all may be comforted.
1 Cor. 14:29-31

One night in 1971 shortly after my wife and I began conducting public meetings in the basement of a Presbyterian Church, a pentecostal woman, pentecostal by experience not denomination, showed up at our meeting and sat in the back. I knew she was going to give another fleshy message in tongues and then interpret her own tongues, just as she had at every other meeting I'd attended when she had been present.

I quickly prayed, "Lord, please don't let her do that in our meeting. I'm pretty new at this and I don't want to have to publicly judge her prophecy if it is off base. Please prevent her from doing her thing."

However, God was about to teach me another lesson. The woman did give a message in tongues, then gave her own interpretation of that message, but when she did, the interpretation broke me to tears. Without a doubt, it was God who had spoken, and I knew it, because the message touched me so deeply that I was moved to tears. In more than twenty-five years that has only happened a very few times. The lesson was: even if you think it may be a donkey speaking, be open: God just might have a word for you!

BE Open to Something New

God may wish to do something totally new with you, or to reveal something you have never even considered. In fact, that is one of the very ways we recognize God's Hand at work, when He does something totally foreign and beyond us in the natural. As an example, a friend of mine by his own admission has never been good at writing. Shortly after receiving salvation and the baptism in the Holy Spirit, he was given a vision in the form of a one-act play with three characters: an unsaved person, a witnessing Christian and the Holy Spirit. Since this was all new to him, he called to ask if this could really have been a revelation from the Lord? He also wondered whether the theology of the vision was sound? It was indeed, and the story line of the play was riveting.

BE Ministering to Him

Thereby continue seeking Him. The men in Acts thirteen heard from the Holy Spirit as they continued ministering and fasting to the Lord.

As they ministered to the Lord, and fasted, the Holy Ghost said. Acts 13:2

BE Hungry

I am hungry. I have an insatiable appetite for God's truth, and desire to daily feed upon the fresh manna of His revelation. The more I seek Him, the more I desire to know.

Blessed are they which do hunger and thirst after righteousness: for they shall be filled. Mat. 5:6

BE Child-Like

Be open and innocent, eager to receive truth, to learn from your loving, patient Father who wishes to instruct you. He will teach whatever He feels to be the best and most appropriate lesson for you.

At that time Jesus answered and said, I thank thee, O Father, Lord of heaven and earth, because thou hast hid these things from the wise and prudent, and hast revealed them unto babes. Mat. 11:25

God has revealed wisdom not unto the worldly wise and prudent, but unto babes. He spoke to more fishermen than Pharisees, because the fishermen were expecting the Messiah. This is an encouragement to become like a little child and simply exercise childlike faith in our loving Father God to give us wisdom.

BE a Lover of the Truth

My only real qualification to hear from God, aside from my hunger, is that I love the truth. I have made the decision to be open to whatever He will give me. What I hear must, of course, stand the tests of Scripture, and the test of logic and common sense, because God is the author of each of these.

Some Christians may be offended to hear a reference connecting God with logic and common sense, thinking that God doesn't have to be logical. He doesn't have to do anything, but He is not the author of confusion, and He is perfectly logical. He created a universe that operates with mathematical precision and logic.

Unfortunately, many people assume that when they become Christians they must 'put their brains in a sack and throw them out the window.' As a result, they gullibly believe that anything said by anyone who stands before them professing to be a Christian, professing to be speaking for God or about God, is infallible. WRONG! And so the Scripture warns:

Beloved, believe not every spirit, but try the spirits whether they are of God: because many false prophets are gone out into the world. 1 John 4:1

BE Totally Honest

Be willing to test and try the revelation you receive with other Scripture. Be willing to be proven wrong. But keep on seeking until you are sure. Make yourself like the Bereans, about whom it was written:

Unto Berea...These were more noble...in that they received the word with all readiness of mind, and searched the scriptures daily, whether those things were so. Acts 17:11

Be careful to avoid pride, because

Knowledge puffeth up, but charity edifieth. And if any man think that he knoweth any thing, he knoweth nothing yet as he ought to know. 1 Cor. 8:1b,2

BE Humble

Remain humble, do not let pride gain a foothold. Be willing to question the leadings you receive; be willing to test and try the spirits; be willing to be proven wrong.

Be not wise in thine own eyes: fear the Lord and depart from evil. Prov. 3:7

We must learn to humbly and fully depend upon God and rely upon Him for revelation and guidance.

Trust in the Lord with all thine heart; and lean not unto thine own understanding. In all thy ways acknowledge him, and he shall direct thy paths. Prov. 3:5-6

Trust in the Lord and not in yourself; do not put your trust in princes, kings nor the wisdom of man.

The fear of the Lord is the instruction of wisdom; and before honour is humility. Prov. 15:33

Lord, thou hast heard the desire of the humble: thou wilt prepare their heart, thou wilt cause thine ear to hear.

Psa. 10:17

BE Not Discouraged

Make the decision that you will not give up, and will trust God for the answer no matter how long it takes, until He chooses to reveal the mystery to you. I have often shared with the people at our Thursday night meetings that I didn't know what God meant or didn't fully understand a particular passage, but I was excited by discovering the question, because I knew He would eventually reveal it to us. Formulating the question creates a handle or a link, between us and the Source of Answers.

Be Ready

Be prepared; use self-discipline. Daniel and his companions were ready for their roles in captivity because they had applied themselves while in Jerusalem. They were ready. We must also be ready. Be "on fire" for God; "that which has been kindled is always ready." Keep a hunger for God's truth burning in your heart.

BE Thoughtful, a Ponderer

Be thoughtful, look around, try to see and consider the alternatives, and different viewpoints. Ponder the things

God shows you, as Daniel pondered his questions and God's truth.

I kept the matter in my heart. Dan. 7:28

BE Thankful

If God gives part of the answer, thank Him for it. Then meditate and chew on what He has given to you until He gives you more. You may get a seemingly illogical Scripture or interpretation. For example, God might quicken to you this verse as He did to a childless couple after we prayed for them. *He maketh the barren woman...to be a joyful mother of children*. Psa. 113:9 That couple received that Scripture as a promise from the Lord and subsequently had four children.

Hunger exists in the heart. This is similar to that God-shaped vacuum hunger you've heard about, but even after that initial heart-hunger is filled, there remains an on-going-hunger for more of God - especially for more of God's truth!

-- Our Prayer --

Father, forgive me for being among those who are described by You in this passage, "For this people's heart is waxed gross, and their ears are dull of hearing, and their eyes they have [willfully] closed; lest at any time they should see with their eyes and hear with their ears, and should understand with their heart, and should be converted, and I should heal them." (Mat. 13:15)

How God May Speak to us

As you seek to tune in to God, keep in mind that God's voice may come to us through other men. He may choose to give you truth, revelation, and wisdom through pastors, prophets, evangelists, teachers, friends, elders, more mature believers, or counselors

Realize, also that The Word of God is the voice of God! Most often His voice will come to us, expressed through His Word. Whichever way it comes, remember these great truths: The voice of God...

will always agree with the Word of God!
will never be in contradiction to Word of God!
will always exalt Jesus!
will hold Him in reverence!
will never diminish His importance!

God's Word is His voice! For those who reject his voice, or cannot hear it, God has made a provision of signs.

And it shall come to pass, if they will not believe thee, neither hearken to the voice of the first sign, that they will believe the voice of the latter sign. Exo. 4:8

If thou wilt diligently hearken to the voice of the Lord thy God, and wilt do that which is right in his sight, and wilt give ear to his commandments, and keep all his statutes, I will put none of these diseases upon thee, which I have brought upon the Egyptians: for I am the Lord that healeth thee. Exo. 15:26

And after the earthquake a fire; but the Lord was not in the fire: and after the fire a still small voice. 1 Ki. 19:12

The Holy Spirit comments that God sometimes speaks in a still (quiet), small (soft, inner) voice. This is probably the most commonly experienced form of hearing God, the gentle inward nudging, or knowing, within your soul as it is touched by His Spirit.

God's voice may also come to us through

The **words** (mouths) of two or more witnesses,

Dreams,

Circumstances,

Confirming signs, such as details surprisingly falling into place, and doors being mysteriously opened for you.

Confirmations, can even come from mouths of unbelievers, an accidentally overheard conversation, a direct statement from a stranger or someone without any way of knowing about the question on your heart.

Revelations, such as a song brought to mind, a word or a thought recalled, or an image brought to mind

Visions are still given today also.

Remember that God's word is God's voice, speaking to your heart! My prayer is that this book will serve as a spiritual appetizer for you, that it stimulates your own appetite for God's truth!

I have found that my greatest personal encouragement comes from having discovered the truth that God Is a Perfect Communicator.

God Is a Perfect Communicator

I realize that I'm not a perfect listener; I'm not a perfect pupil, but I do have a perfect Teacher, *a Perfect Communicator*. He can communicate to me even if I'm a poor hearer. If he can even speak through the mouth of a donkey when no other mouth was available to Him, then He can certainly manage to communicate with you and me. I take great comfort from the fact that God has in the past supernaturally used a donkey as a spokesman to communicate his truth. It builds my faith that even I might be used as a mouthpiece for Him. I suspect that as a man, and especially as a child of His, I am a more willing and fitting instrument for His use.

Remember the basic principle: our God is a perfect communicator! I am not, nor do I need to be, a perfect listener, because He is a perfect communicator!

You have probably had the experience while driving down a country highway, of passing a local radio station and having its broadcast signal overpower the station you were listening to. The power of that station was sufficient to overcome your radio's tuning, and cause you to pick up its signal. You didn't choose to listen to that station, but because of your proximity and its power, it caused you to hear its signal.

How much more is God capable of causing His desired message to be heard by any ear, and especially the ear of any one who is desirous, or willing to hear His message! God is able to communicate with you.

If any man will do his will, he shall know of the doctrine, whether it be of God, or whether I speak of myself.

John 7:17

I have talked with hundreds of people who fear that they are unable to hear God's voice, or that they have not heard the right voice when they actually have!

The truth of God as Perfect Communicator produces faith to take a further step, to be used by God to speak to others about him, and a parenthetic BE.

BE a Faithful Witness

Contrary to much modern teaching, God did not call us to be supersalesmen. He called us to be witnesses. He said that by virtue of our receiving an empowering from the Holy Spirit, we would automatically be His witnesses.

But ye shall receive power, after that the Holy Ghost is come upon you: and ye shall be witnesses unto me both in Jerusalem, and in all Judaea, and in Samaria, and unto the uttermost part of the earth. Acts 1:8

What is expected of a witness in a court of law? He simply tells the truth when the judge gives him an opportunity to do so. That sounds mundane, but it is the truth.

Many years ago I made "a deal" with the Lord. Upon returning from a ministry trip, I felt condemnation for not witnessing to the person seated next to me on the flight home. No opportunity had arisen to witness or even to have a meaningful conversation. I told the Lord that I would be happy to witness to anyone but that I wasn't capable of determining who was ready or willing to receive a message. I proposed a partnership; that I would only share with people who first opened a conversation with me. If the stranger asked a question or started a conversation in any way, I would give him all he was willing to accept. If he did not open the conversation, I would rest, nap, or read without condemnation.

On my very next flight, the woman next to me asked "What kind of Bible is that you're reading?" I closed it and witnessed to her for the rest of the flight. I told the truth, when the Judge gave me the opportunity. My wife used to laugh and say that she could always spot the women who had been sitting next to me on the plane, because when they got off, their mascara was streaked down their cheeks.

-- Our Prayer --

O Lord God, give us hearing ears and willing hearts to receive the messages which You desire to speak to us.

CHAPTER SIX

THE NUMBERS OF WISDOM

Someone has said we are no longer living in the Book of Numbers, but are now living in the Book of Acts, the only book without a close. However, numbers abound in The Book, and their dramatic significance is being revealed in this late hour to various men of God!

The Holy Spirit spoke through the Apostle John on the Isle of Patmos,

Here is wisdom. Let him that hath understanding count the number of the beast: for it is the number of a man; and his number is Six hundred threescore and six. Rev. 13:18

The interpretation and identity of the beast I leave to others. However, even without that identification, wisdom is contained in this verse. The Holy Spirit states the number of the beast spells out the name of a man, therefore the Word of God holds more than the words themselves, there may also be encoded messages. This is a clear introduction to the subject of gematria, which is the system of utilizing the numerical values of the Hebrew or Greek letters to translate or transpose numbers to letters, or vice versa.

A similar passage is found in Revelation 17:9.

And here is the mind which hath wisdom. The seven heads are seven mountains, on which the woman sitteth.

The Spirit is stating that the seven heads represents the seven hills of Rome which was referred to as "the city on seven hills" by many of the early historians and writers including Julius Caesar. Thus actual numbers in Scripture may not only be symbolic, but can also represent or identify specific things, people and places.

More information exists within the Word of God than we might imagine. In recent years men working independently around the world have discovered amazing mathematical values hidden within the Scripture which confirm the supernatural origin of the Word of God. Many have observed the repetitions of the pattern of sevens within Scripture. J.R. Church has written a brilliant work, *The Mystery of the Menorah*, in which He shows the Scriptures of the Old Testament were written following the pattern of the seven-candled Menorah lamp, and those of the New Testament follow the pattern of the nine-candled Hanukkah Menorah. (i.e. nine gifts of the Spirit; nine fruit of the Spirit) Around the turn of the century Panin discovered and it was confirmed by others, that the sum of the values of all the letters in chapters and verses proved the Divine authorship of the written Word.

There is also a concept referred to as equidistant letter sequences, or ELS for short, which was first taken seriously in 1988 after a paper was presented and published by three mathematical statisticians from the Hebrew University and the Jerusalem College of Technology. They discovered that words were encoded in the Hebrew Biblical texts which could not have occurred by accident, nor been placed there by human effort. In testing their theory, they found the names of thirty-four of the most important Jewish heroes encoded in the text.

Key

Truth

Truth

I obtained from the author a copy of his new book entitled *Yeshua, The Hebrew Factor* by Yacov A. Rambsel, a Bible scholar and the pastor of a Messianic congregation. Searching in a similar vein, Pastor Rambsel made numerous startling ELS discoveries. For example, he discovered encoded: *Yeshua shmi* or "Yeshua is my name," identifying the Suffering Servant by name within the text in the familiar Messianic passage, Isaiah 53:10,

Yet it pleased the Lord to bruise him; he hath put him to grief: when thou shalt make his soul an offering for sin, he shall see his seed, he shall prolong his days, and the pleasure of the Lord shall prosper in his hand.

In the familiar prophetic passage, foretelling the place of the Saviour's birth,

But thou, Bethlehem Ephratah, though thou be little among the thousands of Judah, yet out of thee shall he come forth unto me that is to be ruler in Israel; whose goings forth have been from of old, from everlasting. Micah 5:2

Pastor Rambsel found the word *Yeshua* encoded, revealing who would come from there. In fact he found the name of Jesus, *Yeshua*, encoded in the first verse of Genesis; Psalm 22, the crucifixion psalm; and again in the passage from Daniel, which mentions the time when *shall Messiah be cut off*, plainly identifying who the Messiah is.

Other Messianic prophecies are also encoded with a name of the Messiah, removing any doubt of coincidence.

Therefore the Lord himself shall give you a sign; Behold, a virgin shall conceive, and bear a son, and shall call his name Immanuel. Isa. 7:14

Most Christians recognize the Jewish phrase or title, *Yeshua ha'Mashiac* meaning Jesus the Messiah. In this passage the word *Mashiac* is encoded, internal confirmation that the virgin's son shall be the Messiah.

Jesus' Hebrew name of *Yeshua* also appears encoded in one of the most startling prophetic passages of the Old Testament.

Who hath ascended up into heaven, or descended? who hath gathered the wind in his fists? who hath bound the waters in a garment? who hath established all the ends of the earth? what is his name, and ***what is his son's name****, if thou canst tell?*

Encoded in this passage in the original Hebrew letters starting at *yod* and counting every twenty-second letter from right to left, as Hebrew is read, is the encoded message, *Yeshua shai* which means "Yeshua, the gift." The word *Yeshua* is found a second time backwards in the same verse.

Even without Rambsel's great depth of knowledge of Hebrew and gematria, we can find wisdom. In the following verse is a reference to "the Rod." The answer to the clue is in Isaiah. 11:1.

The Lord's voice crieth unto the city, and the man of wisdom shall see thy name: hear ye the rod, and who hath appointed it.

Micah 6:9

God, is the Great Mathematician, and has chosen to operate His universe according to mathematical principles, and laws, such as gravity. The seven notes make possible the infinite musical octave variations of harmonies and symphonies. The eighth note is just the beginning of the next octave; same notes only higher. Seven in the Scriptures is perfection or completeness, and eight the number indicating a new beginning, as the first day of the next week. The days of the week established in Genesis indicate the same pattern.

In this age we should not be surprised by encoded messages. Everyone who has used a computer should realize that when one types a letter, the screen merely shows the words of the letter. However, there are hundreds of specially encoded messages which are not visible but give directions to set the page length, margins, size and style of type and control the printer. If man can add encoded messages to his writing, it should not be amazing for the One who created language and all communication, to use them for His purposes.

God has placed the mysteries and hidden revelations in His written Word. He, alone, can now reveal to us their mysterious meanings. It is exciting to know that He wills to do so!

-- Our Prayer --

Lord, It is You Who have placed the mysteries and hidden revelations in the written Word of God; only You can reveal these mysteries and their meanings. We thank You for the expression of Your will to do so! Amen

CHAPTER SEVEN

GOD'S REASONS FOR REVEALING HIDDEN TRUTHS

God chooses to give wisdom, knowledge and understanding so that man will be better equipped to communicate with Him. When He created Adam, He gave the gift of a new language, which Adam did not have to learn. As a part of His plan of restoration of fallen man He did the same for the new group of believers at Pentecost. Once again He gave the gift of a new undefiled language with which they could praise, magnify and communicate with Him!

The time is coming soon when all things shall be revealed. This must occur before the end of this present age. Every secret will be revealed. Every mystery will be made known.

There was a time when *the whole earth was of one language, and of one speech.* (Gen. 11:1) The men in that day decided to make a name for themselves, and in an attempt to be independent of God, they began a building project. God responded by holding a summit meeting of the Godhead saying, *let us go down, and there confound their language, that they may not understand one another's speech.* (Gen. 11:7) Confusion of language which caused men to be separated and scattered was a judgment from God.

God united man (i.e., believers - the church) with a new language. Just as Adam received the gift of a language for communication with God, God has given to believers the opportunity to receive His Spirit and a new pure, and undefiled language of perfect praise which doesn't need to be learned, and with which they may now worship the Father, as Jesus promised.

But the hour cometh, and now is, when the true worshippers shall worship the Father in spirit and in truth: for the Father seeketh such to worship him. John 4:23

God loves to reveal Himself, His will, His word, His counsels, His plans and purposes to those whom He knows are willing to receive His truth. God does not want His revelation to remain hidden.

God's purpose in revealing His truth is stated as,

What I tell you in darkness, that speak ye in light: and what ye hear in the ear, that preach ye upon the housetops.
Mat. 10:27

Truth is revealed so it can be proclaimed, taught, or shared with others in the body. Use the revelation granted to you. Matthew 10:27 reiterates that secrets are revealed during the night (darkness).

Hast thou heard the secret of God? and dost thou restrain wisdom to thyself? Job 15:8

Job implied that revelation is to be shared and that the secret of God is wisdom.

However, the most important purpose of revelation is that we might come to more fully know God as God, and understand more fully who He is.

And I will give thee the treasures of darkness, and hidden riches of secret places, that thou mayest know that I, the Lord, which call thee by thy name, am the God of Israel.
Isa. 45:3

God's desire in this end-time era is to unveil everything cloaked in mystery:

I will utter things which have been kept secret from the foundation of the world. Mat. 13:35

For there is nothing covered, that shall not be revealed; and hid, that shall not be known. Mat. 10:26

But God hath revealed them unto us by his Spirit: for the Spirit searcheth all things, yea, the deep things of God.
1 Cor. 2:10

Paul included an important clue in his verse: one must yield to the Spirit because the Spirit is God's Revealer of deep things. The believer must come to the point of wanting God and a relationship with His Spirit more than reputation, dignity or any other thing that would hold him back from a complete surrender to God, of body, soul and spirit, that includes our most unruly member, the tongue, which no man can tame.

God has diverse purposes for dreams, revelations, and visions which are illustrated and directly stated throughout the Scriptures. These communications continue with the body of believers today as God, who does not change, continues to instruct His people.

God Answers Questions

God will answer our questions as He did those of Daniel and another Bible hero, Gideon. When the latter was addressed by the angel of the Lord, as a *mighty man of valour*, and told that he would save Israel, Gideon doubted his own qualifications.

And he said unto him, Oh my Lord, wherewith shall I save Israel? behold, my family is poor in Manasseh, and I am the least in my father's house. Judg. 6:15

I'm a nobody, how can this be? God answered him in a fleece. (Fleeces can be abused but are scriptural. When God promises something totally unbelievable, a fleece may be appropriate, but not merely to satisfy curiosity.) Then Gideon "accidentally" overheard the relating of a dream and its interpretation.

And when Gideon was come, behold, there was a man that told a dream unto his fellow, and said, Behold, I dreamed a dream, and, lo, a cake of barley bread tumbled into the host of Midian, and came unto a tent, and smote it that it fell, and overturned it, that the tent lay along. And his fellow answered and said, This is nothing else save the sword of Gideon the son of Joash, a man of Israel: for into his hand hath God delivered Midian, and all the host. And it was so, when Gideon heard the telling of the dream, and the interpretation thereof, that he worshipped...and said, Arise; for the Lord hath delivered into your hand the host of Midian. Judg. 7:13-15

Notice that the relating of the dream and its interpretation evoked worship from the heart of Gideon, who formerly doubted.

God Edifies, Instructs, Builds-up

Zacharias, although skeptical, was edified when the angel Gabriel revealed the future birth and name of his son, John. Paul wrote that he received by revelation the instructions concerning the Lord's Supper which he describes in the eleventh chapter of First Corinthians, and which is the most frequently read passage at that celebration. Paul was certainly built-up while on board ship, recorded in Acts 27, when he received assurance from an angelic visitor that all aboard would be saved, after *all hope that we should be saved was...taken away.*

Much of our faith is based upon revelation! Salvation itself is based upon a revelation of the reality of Jesus Christ to the heart of a candidate.

God Creates, or Maintains Humility

He thus, keeps from, or warns against, pride.

That he may withdraw man from his purpose, and hide pride from man. Job 33:17

Consider the warning given to King Nebuchadnezzar, and Daniel's interpretation and warning based upon the tree dream in Daniel 3 and 4. When the king refused to heed the warning it came to pass, with the result that

Now I Nebuchadnezzar praise and extol and honour the King of heaven, all whose works are truth, and his ways judgment: and those that walk in pride he is able to abase.
Dan. 4:37

God Sets People Free from Bondage

The Scriptures chronicle many people protected and delivered from bondages both physical and spiritual, as the result of information supernaturally imparted such as Shadrach, Meshach, and Abednego, Daniel, Nebuchadnezzar, the wise men, Joseph, and the Holy family. The Lord continues to work the same way today. Individuals in our prayer room often have had either their need for deliverance or the solution made known to them in dreams or revelation.

One such young woman returned to our prayer room seeking deliverance from the recurrence of an eating disorder. She began to explain why she returned for prayer. "I seemed to be completely free after being prayed for and have had several good weeks, but my problem has returned and I think I may have a clue. I have had a strange dream. In this dream I saw out of the corner of my eye, something very frightening, black and ugly, jump onto my back from a figure whom I understood to be my mother. I feel there is a connection."

It turned out there was. Her mother had faced starvation as a child living in Germany during World War Two and had picked up a spirit of the fear of starvation. This spirit, which had tormented her mother through out her life, had somehow been passed on to her daughter. It was cast out and the daughter has now been completely free of the recurrence of her problem for nearly ten years.[7]

Twenty-six years ago I would not have been able to receive any guidance concerning deliverance, because I didn't believe in it. My mind was closed to the possibility of demons existing today. Our theology, traditions and preconceived ideas put limitations upon God, to the extent that we are not open to hear Him speak, as He said of some whose, *ears are dull of hearing, and their eyes they have closed.* (Mat. 13:15) He indicates there was on their part a willful rejection of the truth which He would offer.

God Reveals and Convicts of Previously Unrecognized Sin(s)

One of Holy Spirit's roles is to convict of sin. An example is seen with the first righteous curse in Scripture, upon Abimelech in Genesis chapter 20.

But God came to Abimelech in a dream by night, and said to him, Behold, thou art but a dead man, for the woman which thou hast taken; for she is a man's wife.

Gen. 20:3

Now therefore restore the man his wife; for he is a prophet, and he shall pray for thee, and thou shalt live: and if thou

[7] The daughter actually had a second spirit of the fear of starvation, passed to her from her mother.

restore her not, know thou that thou shalt surely die, thou, and all that are thine. Gen. 20:7

Abraham had told the king that Sarah was his sister, which was only half the truth. The revelation in the dream saved Sarah and the lineage of faith from destruction and saved the life of the heathen king as well.

A beautiful example of this principle, that it is the Holy Spirit's task to convict of sin, was made very real to me recently. I had the privilege of ministering to a man who had been a Buddhist for twenty-six years.

As I began explaining salvation to him, He asked, "Was my being a Buddhist a sin? Every Christian I have talked to has tried to convince me it was a sin. How could it have been a sin, when I was trying to find God?"

"You're asking the wrong person. It is the Holy Spirit's job to convict you of sin. If it was sin, let Him tell you, I won't."

The answer seemed to satisfy him and he allowed me to continue. Finally, I prepared to lead him in a sinner's prayer. I began the prayer slowly, allowing him time to repeat the words after me. He commenced his prayer adding the words, "Lord Jesus, forgive me for being a Buddhist."

The Holy Spirit had done His part, when I, for once, had the good sense to be still and let Him do the convicting portion of the salvation process.

God Saves Lives

The most familiar dream that provided escape was Joseph's which directed him to take Mary and Jesus to Egypt.

Behold, the angel of the Lord appeareth to Joseph in a dream, saying, Arise, and take the young child and his mother, and flee into Egypt, and be thou there until I bring thee word: for Herod will seek the young child to destroy him. Mat. 2:13

The life of Jesus was spared as a result of this dream. The life of Abimelech was also saved by a dream, as were the lives of Daniel, Shadrach, Meshach, and Abednego by the interpretation of the unremembered dream in Daniel 2:1.

God Provides Divine Guidance

O Lord, I know that the way of man is not in himself: it is not in man...to direct his steps. Jer. 10:23

Man erroneously follows his own path to destruction, but God graciously grants guidance.

That he may withdraw man from his [own] *purpose.*
Job 33:17a

God's direction to Joseph to take his family to Egypt was supernatural guidance spoken by an angel in the dream.

God Warns of Unperceived Dangers

God spoke to the wise men by means of a dream.

And being warned of God in a dream that they should not return to Herod, they departed into their own country another way. Mat. 2:12

Daniel's interpretations of Nebuchadnezzar's dreams were also warnings of his judgement.

God Speaks to His Children

God is a good father, and God is Love. Speaking is an act of love. The cruelest thing one can do to a child is to ignore him. God isn't cruel. He is compassionate and desires to have a relationship with you. You were created to have a relationship with Him.

When we talk with God we discover why are we here.

CHAPTER EIGHT

WHY ARE WE HERE?

Man has a void for God, which God has made provision to fill.

Deep calleth unto deep. Psa. 42:7

Several years ago I interviewed a ninety-one-year-old saint, who had formerly been a medical missionary and lifelong Bible teacher. She suddenly interjected into our conversation, "Bill, man has always wanted to know the answer to that old question, Why am I here? I can tell you: **The reason man is here is to grow his spirit; to prepare himself for heaven.**"

My spirit responded immediately. Her answer was even more specific than the Presbyterian catechism's answer which I have always liked. "The chief end of man is to glorify God and to enjoy Him forever."

God's purpose for man from the beginning has been to have fellowship and be a co-worker with Him, caring for His garden, and repopulating the earth: while being developed into *a manchild in the image and likeness of God,* and of Jesus Christ, *until Christ be formed in you* (Gal. 4:19). This individual development parallels the formation and growth of His church; the creation of a people for Himself, in God's own image and likeness.

God is our Father and has a father's desire for His sons to succeed. Our success also brings honor to Him. He desires maturity in His offspring, that we might also mature and become like Him.

Be ye therefore perfect, even as your Father which is in heaven is perfect. Mat. 5:48

He wants us to accurately reflect and represent His kingdom, as His ambassadors. To that end Paul prayed, and Jesus encouraged,

That I may know him, and the power of his resurrection, and the fellowship of his sufferings, being made conformable unto his death. Phil. 3:10

I am the vine, ye are the branches: He that abideth in me, and I in him, the same bringeth forth much fruit: for without me ye can do nothing. If ye abide in me, and my words abide in you, ye shall ask what ye will, and it shall be done unto you. Herein is my Father glorified, that ye bear much fruit; so shall ye be my disciple. John 15:5,7-8

But seek ye first the kingdom of God, and his righteousness; and all these things shall be added unto you.
Mat. 6:33

How do we do that? How do we grow our spirit and prepare ourselves for Heaven? First, we employ the seeking, asking Keys which we have discovered and then submit fully to God. We must grow in grace and increase in our knowledge of Him, as Peter prayed for the believers to whom he wrote,

But grow in grace, and in the knowledge of our Lord and Saviour Jesus Christ. 2 Pet. 3:18a

Grace and peace be multiplied unto you through the knowledge of God, and of Jesus our Lord, According as his divine power hath given unto us all things that pertain unto life and godliness, through the knowledge of him that hath called us to glory and virtue: Whereby are given unto us exceeding great and precious promises: that by these ye might be partakers of the divine nature, having escaped the corruption that is in the world through lust. 2 Pet. 1:2-4

For if these things be in you, and abound, they make you that ye shall neither be barren nor unfruitful in the knowledge of our Lord Jesus Christ. 2 Pet. 1:8

The second step is fellowship with God, spending time with Him.

God desires to spend time fellowshipping with man. This is not a concept devised by man, as we might imagine, but rather is in accordance with God's divine purpose and plan. The initial evidence for this is in Genesis.

In Genesis 2:8-10 the goodness of God was demonstrated toward His created beings. He provided everything they needed, food was merely plucked and eaten, and fresh water was delivered to their garden home. God also recognized the propensity of man, made in God's own image and likeness, for loneliness. To accommodate his need for companionship and for someone to love, He made a helpmate for Adam. (Gen. 2:20-22)

And the Lord God said, It is not good that the man should be alone; I will make him an help meet for him.
Gen. 2:18

If Adam was created in the image and likeness of God, then logically God, like Adam, must have an inherent need for fellowship, therefore He made Adam to fulfill His own desire for fellowship, just as He later made Eve to be the object of Adam's love.

God from the beginning intended for man to be a co-laborer with Him. After God created all the other animals to inhabit the planet, Adam performed a feat of phenomenal creativity when he named all the animals. Adam obviously was endowed with an enormous capacity for creative thought, in addition to the gift and grasp of a language to effectively communicate with God.

God met with Adam and Eve every morning.

And they heard the voice of the Lord God walking in the garden in the cool of the day. Gen. 3:8a

During these pleasant times of fellowship, God probably revealed truths directly to Adam. Josephus wrote that God gave the pre-flood people such long lives so that they might perfect their understanding of astronomy. He attributed the source of astronomy to the family of Seth, while other even earlier sources in Arabia and Persia attributed it variously to Adam, Seth or Enoch.

Adam and his wife hid themselves from the presence of the Lord God amongst the trees of the garden. And the Lord God called unto Adam, and said unto him, Where art thou?
Gen. 3:9

God was faithful to His apparent appointment to meet with man, even if man was not faithful. Of course, God, by virtue of His foreknowledge, knew that Adam was hiding among the trees. Adam had his first experience with stomach-knotting fear as he attempted to hide from His Great Benefactor. Yet God, being longsuffering, merciful and patient, and because of His great love for His children, called out to summon Adam back into fellowship. God desired to give him an opportunity to repent, and to be restored to fellowship.

The Lord's Supper is a tangible memorial of the fellowship desired by God. The memorial is a meal of hospitality, itself a covenant. We have shared the hospitality of Jesus in the Communion meal, it's pattern hosted by Him in person. That pattern was a reminder that God has in the past, and will again, choose to break bread with and have fellowship with man, those who are His followers, the believers, His people. We look forward to that glorious day in the not-too-distant future when we shall sit down with Him at the Marriage Supper of the Lamb.

Praise God!

CHAPTER NINE

THE AMAZING SYMBOLISM OF
DANIEL CHAPTER SIX

THE SECRET OF DANIEL IN THE LION'S DEN

Who Was in The Lion's Den?

The more we know of the Word of God, the more we understand its symbolism and prophecies. Approaching the Old Testament with the hindsight of the New Testament and unfolding historical events is like reading a mystery novel backwards. We have the answers and simply apply them to the various clues or questions. We can readily see where the Author is going with His development of the plot, as we plug the fulfillment into the revelation prophecies. In light of understanding gained in the New Testament and the life and teachings of Jesus, the Messianic prophecies which are contained in the sixth chapter of Daniel become all the more amazing.

Preface

The sixth chapter of Daniel ranks with Isaiah 53 and Psalm 22 for specific Messianic prophesies. This chapter contains facts concerning Daniel which bear unbelievably accurate parallels with the life of Jesus Christ, whom he foreshadows.

Read through the sixth chapter a couple of times before beginning this study to familiarize yourself with the text and to see what the Lord may reveal to you before you consider what He has shown me. Each of the verses from Daniel is included in the text as it is being considered.

Setting the Stage: Babylon and Its Defeat

In that night was Belshazzar the king of the Chaldeans slain. And Darius the Median took the kingdom, being about threescore and two years old. Dan. 5:30-31

Although these verses are direct, they omit the miraculous details by which the Lord brought about the change of power that occurred in one night. This shift in world power set the stage for the events of Daniel six.

When Nebuchadnezzar became ruler of the kingdom of Babylon, he rebuilt the Capitol city of Babylon, making it the most magnificent city of the ancient world, and perhaps of all time. According to Herodotus, the city was 15 miles square. Its walls were 87 feet thick, and 350 feet high (the height of a 35-story building). The walls were wide enough to race six chariots side by side and were topped with 250 lookout towers for protection. Twenty-five magnificent avenues ran east and west, and the same number north and south across the city.

The Euphrates River ran right through the center of the city giving it a limitless water supply. The Great Palace was built in the city's center, on either side of the River. The two halves of the palace were connected by a magnificent bridge and by an underground tunnel passageway.

King Belshazzar was the second ruler of the kingdom of Babylon, under his father Nabonidus who was first ruler, but was elsewhere doing battle to maintain or expand the empire.

Critics have attempted to cast doubt upon the authenticity of the Book of Daniel; because its prophecies are so detailed and accurate, they have to have been given by God, thus critics claimed there was never a King Belshazzar. However, in 1854 a tablet was found confirming the dual rule of Nabonidus and Belshazzar.

At the feast described in chapter five, Belshazzar the playboy king, degenerate, irreverent, and given to drunkenness, was drinking with a thousand of his lords and princes, and their wives and concubines. At the height of their revelry the king committed a God-mocking act of blasphemy. He commanded that the holy vessels captured by Nebuchadnezzar from Jerusalem and the Temple be brought, that they might drink toasts in them to the Babylonian gods, in defiance of the God of Heaven and His power.

He and his counselors were aware the Persian army was gathered outside the walls of their city. Since they considered their city impregnable, they were not concerned. That was not an illogical assumption with walls the height of a 35-story building, 87 feet thick, and men in chariots patrolling on the walls. They should have been safe. Only an act of God could make them vulnerable.

The Persian army under Cyrus was given a brilliant strategy: to drain the River Euphrates so that his army could enter the city on the dried river bed. His plan entailed digging a channel out of sight of the city, to divert the river into a huge lake bypassing the city.

With God's perfect timing Cyrus's attack coincided

with Belshazzar's feast. Cyrus separated his troops into three groups: one diverted the water; the second entered the city under the walls where the Euphrates flowed into the city; the third group entered the city where the Euphrates exited the city.

As soon as the water was low enough to permit, the men started for the center of the city where the palace was located. Due to carelessness, and drunkenness, the guards did not notice the drop in the river's flow nor were the bronze gates lowered and locked to compensate for the dropping water level.

Isaiah prophesied this very occurrence:

That saith to the deep, Be dry, and I will dry up thy rivers: That saith of Cyrus, He is my shepherd, and shall perform all my pleasure: even saying to Jerusalem, Thou shalt be built; and to the temple, Thy foundation shall be laid.

Isa. 44:27-28

Thus saith the Lord to his anointed, to Cyrus, whose right hand I have holden, to subdue nations before him; and I will loose the loins of kings, to open before him the two leaved gates; and the gates shall not be shut; Isa. 45:1

For Jacob my servant's sake, and Israel mine elect, I have even called thee by thy name: I have surnamed thee, though thou hast not known me. Isa. 45:4

One-hundred-seventy-four years beforehand, God gave the name of the one who would deliver Israel from captivity, and details of how the city would be taken. Perhaps, most surprising is that God calls this gentile king, *His anointed* and *His shepherd*. He employed Messianic titles because Cyrus was an archetype of the coming Messiah, in that he would set God's people free, restore the holy city Jerusalem, and bring honor and glory to the true God.

While Belshazzar's great feast was taking place, Nabonidus, who was battling the Persians at Borsippa was beaten back and besieged in a temple where he took refuge until forced to surrender.

All of these events were unknown to the drunken king, but,

In the same hour came forth fingers of a man's hand, and wrote over against the candlestick upon the plaster of the wall of the king's palace: and the king saw the part of the hand that wrote. Then the king's countenance was changed, and his thoughts troubled him, so that the joints of his loins were loosed, and his knees smote one against another. Dan. 5:5-6

When the hand of a man appeared writing like God would write, higher on the wall than a man could reach, the King was filled with terror. "*His loins were loosed*" exactly as Isaiah had prophesied one-hundred-seventy-four years before, and his knees began knocking with fright.

Daniel was at this time an old man, living in obscurity, and unknown to Belshazzar. Yet the queen recommended him, after all the king's wise men proved unable to read the writing. Therefore, Daniel was summoned.

When he arrived, Daniel described to Belshazzar what had taken place before he arrived, obviously by revelation.

Thou...hast lifted up thyself against the Lord of heaven; and...have brought the vessels of his house...and thou, and thy lords, thy wives, and thy concubines, have drunk wine in them; and...praised the gods of silver, and gold, of brass, iron, wood, and stone. Dan. 5:22-23

The following is his interpretation of the message written on the wall:

Then was the part of the hand sent from him; and this writing was written. And this is the writing that was written, MENE, MENE, TEKEL, UPHARSIN.

...MENE; God hath numbered thy kingdom, and finished it.

...TEKEL; Thou art weighed in the balances, and art found wanting.

...PERES;[8] *Thy kingdom is divided, and given to the Medes and Persians.* Dan 5: 24-28

After boldly preaching righteousness to the unrighteous king, Daniel spoke the prophetic interpretation of the writing, that Belshazzar had been judged and found wanting, and that his kingdom would be taken from him and given to the Medes and Persians. Before the sun rose the next morning, Belshazzar was slain and all had come to pass.

His father had been conquered by the Persians; and now the Persian army under Cyrus entered the city undetected, and defeated mighty Babylon. Cyrus, leader of the Persian army, placed Darius the Mede upon the throne of Babylon, perfect prophetic fulfillment almost instantaneously. The miraculous defeat of Babylon, at the end of Daniel five was the end of the prophesied empire of gold described in the second chapter of Daniel, which began with Nebuchadnezzar and ended with the death of his God-mocking grandson, Belshazzar.

8 *Upharsin* and *Peres* are identical; the former is the Chaldean rendering of the word.

The Amazing Similarities Between Jesus and Daniel

A Foreigner Ruled in the Land in Jesus's Day

In the fifteenth year of the reign of Tiberius Caesar, Pontius Pilate being governor of Judaea. Luke 3:1

In Daniel's day, the ruler was Darius who assumed the kingdom and established a new order. In fulfillment of prophecy, he was a Mede appointed by the Persian Cyrus, who had other wars to wage. The new government was not an absolute monarchy, such as Babylon had previously been, but a parliamentary government. The parliament proposed laws which the king then ratified. Once ratified the law could not be changed, according to the laws of the Medes and Persians.

Darius's first recorded act was to establish a hierarchy of authority over the kingdom.

It pleased Darius to set over the kingdom an hundred and twenty princes, which should be over the whole kingdom; And over these three presidents; of whom Daniel was first: that the princes might give accounts unto them, and the king should have no damage. Dan. 6:1-2

Darius's system could be a glimpse into the hierarchy of heaven. As the new kingdom was set up under King Darius, who symbolizes the Godhead, he established three presidents, who correspond to the three Archangels,[9] Gabriel, Michael, and Lucifer. The latter is now fallen and known in his fallen state as Satan. If there are *ruling* angels, there must naturally be other angels subordinated to their rule.

In Daniel the word translated "prince" is Strong's #323 *'achashdarpan* (akh-ash-dar-pan'), of Persian derivation, meaning a satrap or governor of a main province of Persia.

When the word "Prince" refers to the Messiah, it is often, but not exclusively, the Hebrew word *Sar*, (similar to, and pronounced the same as, the Russian word for king or ruler, tsar). In the Hebrew of the Old Testament *tsar* appears in the word "Branch," *naw-tsar*, in Isaiah 11:1 the branch out of the root of Jesse.[10]

And there shall come forth a rod out of the stem of Jesse, and a Branch shall grow out of his roots. Isa. 11:1

In the New Testament, the word "prince" especially when referring to Satan is Strong's #758, *archon* (ar' -khone) from *arche'*; a first (in rank or power): chief (ruler), magistrate prince, ruler.

Thus the Scripture confirms that Satan is indeed the

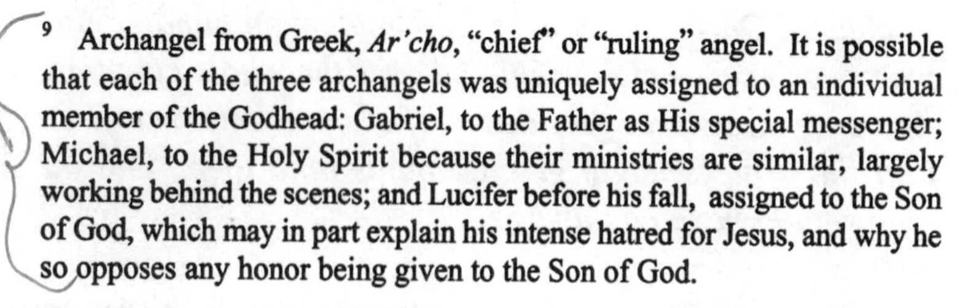

[9] Archangel from Greek, *Ar'cho*, "chief" or "ruling" angel. It is possible that each of the three archangels was uniquely assigned to an individual member of the Godhead: Gabriel, to the Father as His special messenger; Michael, to the Holy Spirit because their ministries are similar, largely working behind the scenes; and Lucifer before his fall, assigned to the Son of God, which may in part explain his intense hatred for Jesus, and why he so opposes any honor being given to the Son of God.

[10] This is developed more fully in the book, *The Heavens Declare...*

missing *arche-angel*, in passages such as the following:

But the Pharisees said, He casteth out devils through the prince of the devils. Mat. 9:34
But when the Pharisees heard it, they said, This fellow doth not cast out devils, but by Beelzebub the prince of the devils. Mat. 12:24
But some of them said, He casteth out devils through Beelzebub the chief of the devils. Luke 11:15
Now is the judgment of this world: now shall the prince of this world be cast out. John 12:31
Hereafter I will not talk much with you: for the prince of this world cometh, and hath nothing in me. John 14:30

Adam was set up by God as a ruler, or governor over planet earth, but he forfeited his dominion to Satan.

Wherein in time past ye walked according to the course of this world, according to the prince of the power of the air, the spirit that now worketh in the children of disobedience. Eph. 2:2

By contrast Jesus is twice identified in Acts as the Prince of life and of salvation, or as Saviour.

Him hath God exalted with his right hand to be a Prince and a Saviour, for to give repentance to Israel, and forgiveness of sins. Acts 5:31

And killed the Prince of life, whom God hath raised from the dead; whereof we are witnesses. Acts 3:15

Under the three presidents Darius established 120 Princes symbolic of the next level of angels who rule over the myriads of angels. One-hundred-twenty is a significant number. Ten is the number symbolizing law, order and government, i.e., *Ten* commandments. This is multiplied by twelve, God's symbolic number representing divine government, i.e., *twelve* Apostles, tribes, thrones.

A clarification of Darius' hierarchy is seen in Daniel 2:49.

Then Daniel requested of the king, and he set Shadrach, Meshach, and Abednego, over the affairs of the province of Babylon: but Daniel sat in the gate of the king.

Daniel was placed above three men who were set over the affairs of the kingdom. These represent the three archangels assigned under Jesus's authority to handle the affairs of the kingdom. It is also interesting to note that only the names of Daniel (corresponding to Jesus), and of Shadrach, Meshach, and Abednego (corresponding to the three archangels) are given in the Scripture, even though they were "among" the Jewish captives, and there were 120 other princes. This parallels the Biblical presentation of the angels: names are only given for the three archangels while all other angels of lower classification remain unnamed, as do the princes in Daniel.

Jesus Began His Kingdom with 120 Subordinates

Jesus' new church was initiated with 120 believers, men and women filled with the Spirit and placed in preeminence over its beginning stage. (Acts 1:15ff)

Jesus Was Given Preeminence

And he is before all things. Col. 1:17

And he is the head of the body, the church: who is the beginning, the firstborn from the dead; that in all things he might have the preeminence. Col. 1:18

God...hath highly exalted him, and given him a name which is above every name. Phil. 2:9

Daniel was preferred above the presidents by the decree of the King, a type of God the Father, thus Daniel symbolizes Jesus, who was placed above the archangels and over the whole kingdom. It was written of both Jesus and Daniel that they were given authority because they had excellent spirits.

Then this Daniel was preferred above the presidents and princes, because an excellent spirit was in him; and the king thought to set him over the whole realm. Dan. 6:3

Jesus Was Beloved of the King of Heaven

Jesus was preferred because He was the Beloved Son of the Father. God the Father audibly endorsed Him as such at the Transfiguration with these words:

This is my beloved Son, in whom I am well pleased; hear ye him. Mat. 17:5

For Daniel to be an archetype, he must not only be beloved of the earthly King as he was, but also beloved of the Father in Heaven, which the angel declared of him.

O Daniel, I am now come forth to give thee skill and understanding...for thou art greatly beloved. Dan. 9:23

O Daniel, a man greatly beloved, understand the words. Dan. 10:11

Jesus Was Hated Without a Cause

Daniel was also hated without a cause. His enemies were not thankful for their own positions which had been granted to them by grace, as gifts from the earthly king.

Jesus Was Opposed Because of Jealousy

Then the presidents and princes sought to find occasion against Daniel concerning the kingdom. Dan. 6:4a

The Babylonian presidents were jealous of Daniel, just as the earthly priests in the kingdom of God were jealous of Jesus, and sought to entrap him. An earlier rebellion, when one third of the heavenly host rebelled against Jesus under Lucifer's leadership is a third example of rebellion or persecution due to envy.

Jesus' Enemies Opposed the Will of God

The Jewish leaders who rejected Jesus were actually rejecting the choice of God; sending Jesus to them was an expression of His will. In similar fashion, the enemies of Daniel plotted a rebellion against the expressed will of the king to honor and exalt his chosen one. Darius' plan was to exalt Daniel, but these enemies, themselves, wanted to be set over all the affairs of the kingdom, instead of Daniel.

Sin Entered the Hearts of Jesus' Enemies

No doubt, someone was the instigator of the plot against Daniel. Just as Lucifer led the rebellion in heaven, there was surely an earthly agitator who was particularly jealous of Daniel, one who thought that the honor and power granted to Daniel should have gone instead to him. In Isaiah's revelation of a pre-world rebellion he indicated that Lucifer envied Jesus' honor.

How art thou fallen from heaven, O Lucifer, son of the morning! how art thou cut down to the ground, which didst weaken the nations! For thou hast said in thine heart, I will ascend into heaven, I will exalt my throne above the stars of God: I will sit also upon the mount of the congregation, in the sides of the north: I will ascend above the heights of the clouds; I will be like the most High. Yet thou shalt be brought down to hell, to the sides of the pit.

Isa. 14:12-15

In the first fulfillment of this prophetic statement, Lucifer was cast *out* and *down* to the region where lions dwell, to the earth. Later he will be cast into a deeper pit, a second fulfillment. Probably Satan desired to have Jesus whom God had exalted and glorified, cast out of heaven, his thinking similar to the strategy of the children's game of "king of the hill." The one who can dislodge the others from the top of the hill becomes "king of the hill."

If that was Satan's plan, the events illustrate God's principle of reversal, returning evil intended against His own, upon the heads of the adversaries of God's people. This principle is a reverse corollary of the Golden Rule and could be called the Just Recompense Rule, and is similar to His law of sowing and reaping. We are to do good as we wish good to be done unto us; those who do evil will have evil returned to them.

The message to both the heavenly and earthly usurpers is clear: How art thou cast down to earth, to a den of lions and finally to the pit. This judgment will be a place

1. of punishment,
2. of death,
3. of fear and torment,
4. of darkness,
5. of destruction,
6. of lions,
7. for bodies to be consumed,
   as were those of the enemies of Daniel.

There may be an irony in the terminology used by Jesus when He prescribed the solution for believers in dealing with Satan and his demonic agents, whom we are to "cast out." When we cast them out "in His name," each time Satan hears the words "cast out" it is an unpleasant reminder of the fact that he has been cast out and soon will be cast down.

In my name shall they cast out devils [demons].

Mark 16:17

Jesus Was Totally Righteous

The Jews were unable to find a just reason to accuse Jesus, as Paul stated:

For...[Jesus]*...was in all points tempted like as we are, yet without sin.* Heb. 4:15

Pilate was unable to find any guilt, in Jesus either.

I find no fault in this man. Luke 23:4

Likewise, the Chaldeans were unable to find any valid basis for accusing Daniel, as is recorded.

But they could find none occasion nor fault; forasmuch as he was faithful, neither was there any error or fault found in him. Dan. 6:4b

Leaders Plot to Kill Jesus

Then assembled together the chief priests, and the scribes, and the elders...And consulted that they might take Jesus by subtlety, and kill him. Mat. 26:3-4

Since the Chaldeans could find no fault either morally or legally in Daniel, they determined to catch him in connection with his faith, or religious observance.

Then said these men, We shall not find any occasion against this Daniel, except we find it against him concerning the law of his God. Dan. 6:5

These men were desperate; for they were typical politicians of their day and profited illegally from their official activities. They also recognized in Daniel a different spirit, an honest spirit, and they knew they would be unable to line their pockets as freely if he governed them.

Leaders Accusing Jesus, Fake Loyalty to Ruler

Then these presidents and princes assembled together to the king, and said thus unto him, King Darius, live for ever.
Dan. 6:6

The Chaldeans greeted their king, hypocritically professed their fealty to the man who ruled over them, "You are our king, may you reign forever."

In like manner, the Jews in Jesus' day falsely professed their allegiance to Caesar before Pilate:

But they cried out, Away with him, away with him, crucify him. Pilate saith unto them, Shall I crucify your King? The chief priests answered, We have no king but Caesar.
John 19:15

Jesus Accused by False Brethren

All the presidents of the kingdom, the governors, and the princes, the counselors, and the captains, have consulted together to establish a royal statute, and to make a firm decree, that whosoever shall ask a petition of any God or man for thirty days, save of thee, O king, he shall be cast into the den of lions. Dan. 6:7

The Jews tried earlier to find a reason to accuse Jesus, but failing, finally suborned false witnesses:

Now the chief priests, and elders, and all the council, sought false witness against Jesus, to put him to death; But found none: yea, though many false witnesses came, yet found they none. At the last came two false witnesses, And said, This fellow said, I am able to destroy the temple of God, and to build it in three days. Mat. 26:59-61

It is an ominous thing for men to set themselves against any man of God; it is likewise ominous to seek the blood of the innocent. Such people often not only seal their own doom, but also pronounce their own sentence.

The presidents and princes had assembled themselves without Daniel. He was not present at their consultation. Shadrach, Meshach, and Abednego were not present either, for they would not have voted for such a proposal. So it was a lie that all were present and agreed. The men of God had not been consulted and had not agreed to such an ungodly decree. These accusers were liars, and thus false witnesses.

Today what they proposed might be called Secular Humanism, which is worship of humankind. It purports that man has the ability to solve all our problems, meet all our needs. Punishment or persecution is decreed for those who choose to disobey and to, instead, worship the God of heaven.

Oddly enough this was a temporary decree, or covenant, for just thirty days, which indicates how sure they were of Daniel's dedication to his God, and how certain they were of making their case within that one-month period.

One wonders why Darius was taken in by this ploy, since their stated goal of deifying Darius was only to last for a period of thirty days. Such is the vanity of man, and indicates how blinding pride can be.

A New Death Penalty in Jesus's Day

The gentiles in Babylon proposed altering an existing law to institute a new kind of death penalty. Their action foreshadows the actions of another gentile nation, Rome, which was responsible for the establishment of martial law just one year prior to the crucifixion of Jesus. Archeologists discovered a stone about thirty years ago, upon which was inscribed the decree of martial law for Jerusalem and all the Jews under Roman rule.

The primary Jewish method of execution for centuries had been stoning, but now a new method of execution was introduced by Rome, that of crucifixion, which by virtue of martial law, superseded their right to stone those they judged worthy of death.

And the scribes and Pharisees brought unto him a woman taken in adultery; and when they had set her in the midst...say unto him...Now Moses in the law commanded us, that such should be stoned: but what sayest thou?
Then took they up stones to cast at him: but Jesus hid himself, and went out of the temple, going through the midst of them, and so passed by. John 8:3-5,59

Stoning was still in effect almost to the time of Jesus's crucifixion, as these passages show. By the time of Stephen's stoning, the martial law edict had been lifted. In the perfection of God's timing, the Jews were not able to stone Jesus, but had to have him crucified, just as David had predicted more than a thousand years earlier in Psalm 22.

Decision of The Ruler Could Not Be Altered

The decree of the ruler was final, and not to be altered.

Pilate answered, What I have written I have written.
John 19:22

Now, O king, establish the decree, and sign the writing, that it be not changed, according to the law of the Medes and Persians, which altereth not. Dan. 6:8

Under the law of the Medes and Persians, once a law had been proposed by the parliament of presidents and princes, and signed by the king, it was fixed and could not be changed, even by the King.

God Does Not Change

We have a God who changeth not, and who does not alter that which He has decreed!

I am the Lord, I change not. Mal. 3:6

The Father... with whom is no variableness. James 1:17

In Daniel 6:8 is a second revelation of Heaven, a picture of God's law which also does not change. Once God's word is spoken, it is forever settled in heaven, eternally!

For ever, O Lord, thy word is settled in heaven.
Psa. 119:89

My covenant will I not break, nor alter the thing that is gone out of my lips. Once have I sworn by my holiness that I will not lie unto David. Psa. 89:34,35

Our hope of eternal life is based upon the Word of God, who cannot (it is impossible for Him to) lie.

In hope of eternal life, which God, that cannot lie, promised before the world began. Titus 1:2

Jesus' Death Officially Decreed in Writing

Pilate wrote the epitaph for Jesus, when he labeled Him as The King of the Jews recorded in Mark. 15:26,

Wherefore king Darius signed the writing and the decree.
Dan. 6:9

The fateful decree was signed for Daniel by Darius, who represents the Father, and it reflects the will of the Father. God who irrevocably agreed (decreed) before this world was formed to let His own Son become *the Lamb slain.*

And all that dwell upon the earth shall worship him, whose names are not written in the book of life of the Lamb slain from the foundation of the world. *Rev. 13:8*

Who verily was foreordained before the foundation of the world, but was manifest in these last times for you.
1 Pet. 1:20

Oh, the unfathomable love, and will of God to bless mankind by sending His Son to earth to die for the world, and especially benefit those who would accept His offer of life eternal. This grand love is expressed repeatedly in beautiful types and symbolism. Two that have blessed me follow.

From the beginning, the Passover lamb (foreshadowing the Lamb of God) was seen on a cross. When a spit is run lengthwise through the body of a lamb, the meat has a tendency to remain in place when the spit is turned. Therefore, a second, transverse spit is run though the shoulders which allows the meat to be turned as it is roasted, picturing in type, the Lamb of God upon the cross.

It makes a cross

Years ago I found a Rabbinic reference to the custom of removing the Passover lamb's intestines and coiling them around the head while roasting. Unbelievably, their minds were blinded to the symbolism; the coiled intestines were called, "Messiah's Crown!"

A second, and most unlikely figure of the Messiah is a serpent upon a pole, but that is indeed a type which Jesus personally confirmed to represent Himself.

And as Moses lifted up the serpent in the wilderness, even so must the Son of man be lifted up: That whosoever believeth in him should not perish, but have eternal life.
John 3:14-15

Jesus applied this unlikely figure to Himself and to the means He would use to provide eternal life on the basis of faith in Himself.

Because of the perfection of God's timing and the unwitting complicity of Rome in passing martial law, the Son of God, was crucified upon a cross. That cross became the Tree of Life by His sacrifice upon it. So that all who partake of its fruit (the blessing resulting from His obedience upon it) shall indeed live forever.

Jesus Ensnared for an Action to Be Performed "In Three Days"

This fellow said, I am able to destroy the temple of God, and to build it in three days. Mat. 26:61

The parliament could find no just basis upon which to accuse Daniel, so his contemporaries devised a plot to ensnare him because of his walk with God, and presented it to King Darius. The Jews' accusation of Jesus was also based upon His walk with God, and concerned something He was going to do in a **three day** period. The Chaldean presidents accused Daniel for what he did **three** times **a day**:

Now when Daniel knew that the writing was signed, he went into his house; and his windows being open in his chamber toward Jerusalem, he kneeled upon his knees three times a day, and prayed, and gave thanks before his God, as he did aforetime. Dan. 6:10

Daniel's custom of praying three times a day was like taking medicine; prayer was applied, or taken, three times per day. Just as one normally takes three meals each day to maintain bodily strength, prayer maintains spiritual strength.

Jesus Continued in Spite of a Death Decree

Although Jesus knew of the death decree, the contract put on His life by the Scribes and Pharisees, he did not cease proclaiming the truth.

Therefore the Jews sought the more to kill him. John 5:18

After these things Jesus walked in Galilee: for he would not walk in Jewry, because the Jews sought to kill him. Did not Moses give you the law, and yet none of you keepeth the law? Why go ye about to kill me? Then said some of them of Jerusalem, Is not this he, whom they (the rulers) *seek to kill?* John 7:1,19,25

Likewise Daniel was aware of the decree, the contract on his life, but did not alter his relationship with God. He continued doing what he felt God wanted him to do, choosing to put his relationship with God above his personal well-being. Both men continued praying and thanking God, even though men of this world were seeking to take their lives.

Jesus Practiced Worship Regularly

And he came to Nazareth, where he had been brought up: and, as his custom was, he went into the synagogue on the sabbath day, and stood up for to read. Luke 4:16

The open window of Daniel's house does not indicate a flagrant flaunting of the law, but rather a continuation of his customary ways. Proof that Daniel's action was not an intentional, rebellious flaunting of the law is seen in the words:

[He] *prayed, and gave thanks before his God, as he did aforetime.* Dan. 6:10

Jesus Submitted His Will to That of The Father

O my Father, if it be possible, let this cup pass from me: nevertheless not as I will, but as thou wilt. Mat. 26:39b

Daniel could have ceased praying to God, could have denied His God, but he did not! He chose to obey God rather than man. The principle involved is stated plainly by

Peter and John when they were confronted by the Jewish rulers after the healing of the man at Gate Beautiful:

And they called them, and commanded them not to speak at all nor teach in the name of Jesus. But Peter and John answered and said unto them, "Whether it be right in the sight of God to hearken unto you more than unto God, judge ye. For we cannot but speak the things which we have seen and heard." Acts 4:18-20

Jesus Taken After Praying Three Times

Then these men assembled, and found Daniel praying and making supplication before his God. Dan. 6:11

Daniel kneeled and prayed to His God three times a day before the open window in his chamber (6:10). The men who were seeking to kill Jesus and assembled against Him, found Him in the place where He regularly prayed. He was in the Garden "*praying and making supplication before his God.*" Jesus had prayed three times.

Jesus Kneeled to Pray

Jesus, like Daniel, who prefigured Him, **kneeled**, and prayed three times in the Garden of Gethsemane:

And he was withdrawn from them about a stone's cast, and ***kneeled*** *down, and prayed.* Luke 22:41

Men Assembled Against Jesus

And he cometh the third time, and saith unto them, Sleep on now, and take your rest: it is enough, the hour is come; behold, the Son of man is betrayed into the hands of sinners. Rise up, let us go; lo, he that betrayeth me is at hand. And immediately, while he yet spake, cometh Judas, one of the twelve, and with him a great multitude with swords and staves, from the chief priests and the scribes and the elders. And they laid their hands on him, and took him.
Mark 14:4-43,46

Men assembled themselves to take Daniel (Dan. 6:11). Jesus was also arrested by a company of men with Judas.

Judas then, having received a band of men (an assembled group) *and officers from the chief priests and Pharisees, cometh thither with lanterns and torches and weapons. Then the band and the captain and officers of the Jews took Jesus, and bound him.*
John 18:3,12

Then took they him, and led him, and brought him into the high priest's house.
Luke 22:54a

Jesus's Enemies Present Case to Ruler

Then they came near, and spake before the king concerning the king's decree; Hast thou not signed a decree, that every man that shall ask a petition of any God or man within thirty days, save of thee, O king, shall be cast into the den of lions? The king answered and said, The thing is true, according to the law of the Medes and Persians, which altereth not.
Dan. 6:12

Both Daniel and Jesus were accused by their enemies of having broken a law deserving of death.

The Jews answered him, We have a law, and by our law ***he ought to die****, because he made himself the Son of God.*
John 19:7

Note also that the Chaldean presidents went to their ruler, King Darius, just as the Jews had to go to Pilate, the Roman ruler, due to the martial law. They could not execute the death penalty without Rome's permission.

Then said Pilate unto them, Take ye him, and judge him according to your law. The Jews therefore said unto him, It is not lawful for us to put any man to death. John 18:31

Jesus Betrayed for 30...

The evil men assembling before Darius foreshadow Judas. Evil men in Daniel's day covenanted with the king for thirty days in which they would betray Daniel. The period of time leading to the death sentence on Daniel was **thirty** days, the price paid to Judas for the betrayal of Jesus unto death was **thirty** pieces of silver.

Judas covenanted with the Jewish rulers for thirty pieces of silver to betray Jesus, the ransom price for a dead slave. Silver is both the medium of, and the symbol of, redemption in the Bible.

If the ox shall push a manservant or a maidservant; he shall give unto their master thirty shekels of silver, and the ox shall be stoned. Exo. 21:32

And I said unto them, If ye think good, give me my price; and if not, forbear. So they weighed for my price thirty pieces of silver. And the Lord said unto me, Cast it unto the potter: a goodly price that I was prised at of them. And I took the thirty pieces of silver, and cast them to the potter in the house of the Lord. Zec. 11:12-13

The price paid to Judas for arranging the death of Jesus was that established for a dead servant, a dead servant gored by an ox, or "rheem." Satan is often symbolically pictured as a rushing rheem or horned bull.[11]

Jesus Faced His Trials Alone

Jesus was betrayed by one of His fellows and all His followers deserted Him.

Then saith Jesus unto them, All ye shall be offended because of me this night: for it is written, I will smite the shepherd, and the sheep of the flock shall be scattered abroad. Mat. 26:31

And they all forsook him, and fled. Mark 14:50

But all this was done, that the scriptures of the prophets might be fulfilled. Then all the disciples forsook him, and fled. Mat. 26:56

[11] In the gospel written in the stars of heaven, the tip of one of the bull's horns is seen to be piercing the heel of the Messiah. See *The Heavens Declare...*

Both men were forsaken by their associates and left to face their fates of trials and sufferings alone, without human aid. There is no mention of Shadrach, Meshach, and Abed-nego; they may have been engaging in the king's business elsewhere, but whatever the reason, they were not present to comfort or encourage Daniel.

Jesus Was a Judean

Jesus was a Judean by birth, and by residence a citizen of Galilee. Daniel was a *child of Judah,* i.e., although elderly at this point, had been among the children taken captive in Judah.

Now when Jesus was born in Bethlehem of Judaea in the days of Herod the king, behold, there came wise men from the east to Jerusalem. Mat. 2:1

Now in the fifteenth year of the reign of Tiberius Caesar, Pontius Pilate being governor of Judaea, and Herod being tetrarch of Galilee. Luke 3:1a

Jesus Was Born During Captivity of Judah

Then answered they and said before the king, That Daniel, which is of the children of the captivity of Judah, regardeth not thee, O king, nor the decree that thou hast signed, but maketh his petition three times a day. Dan. 6:13

Jesus like Daniel was born while His own nation was subject to the outrageous treatment of a violent, conquering gentile nation.

Jesus Accused of Rebellion Against Gentile King

His contemporaries accused Daniel of flaunting the king's authority and worshiping his own god instead. So did the Jews of a later era bring similar charges against another Son of Judah. The Jews falsely charged Jesus with rebellion against an earthly king, just as Daniel had been.

And they began to accuse him, saying, We found this fellow perverting the nation... Luke 23:2

The Ruler's Wife Praises Jesus

When he was set down on the judgment seat, his wife sent unto him, saying, Have thou nothing to do with that just man: for I have suffered many things this day in a dream because of him. Mat. 27:19

Something similar occurred when the Queen interceded with Belshazzar in behalf of Daniel, of whom she said:

There is a man...in whom is the spirit of the holy gods...an excellent spirit, and knowledge, and understanding, interpreting of dreams...let Daniel be called... and he will show the interpretation. Dan 5:11-12

Ruler Wanted to Release Jesus

Then the king, when he heard these words, was sore displeased with himself, and set his heart on Daniel to deliver him. Dan. 6:14a

And he laboured till the going down of the sun to deliver him. Dan. 6:14b

Darius was angry with himself for being tricked into signing the decree. It is written that Pilate recognized the motives of Jesus' betrayers.

For he knew that for envy they had delivered him.
Mat. 27:18

And from thenceforth Pilate sought to release him.
John 19:12a

Pilate attempted to find a way to release Jesus at least three different ways over the better part of a day. First Pilate tried to give Jesus an opportunity to defend Himself, but Jesus made no response to the accusations of the Jewish rulers. (Mat. 27:12) Pilate tried to get Jesus to give a defense, when he asked Jesus "Don't you hear all their charges?" (Mat. 27:13) Pilate adjudged Him to be innocent three times declaring to the Jewish rulers, "I find no fault in Him." (Luk. 23:4)

When he tried to send Jesus to Herod, Herod sent Him back. (Luk. 23:7) Pilate tried to release Jesus to the Jews, but they chose Barabbas. When they cried "Crucify Jesus," he asked the crowd, "Why? What evil has he done?" In other words, Pilate considered Jesus innocent. Attempting to absolve himself, Pilate washed his own hands, disavowing any involvement in the proceedings. (cf. Deut. 21:6-9)

Then released he Barabbas unto them: and when he had scourged Jesus, he delivered him to be crucified.
Mat. 27:26

Pilate had Jesus scourged, within one lash of a death sentence (forty lashes was considered a death penalty, and prevented re-punishment for the same offense, under the principle of "double jeopardy") in hopes of appeasing their wrath, and so,

Said unto them, ye have brought this man unto me, as one that perverteth the people: and, behold, I, having examined him before you, have found no fault in this man touching those things whereof ye accuse him. Luke 23:14

Pilate...said...I find in him no fault at all. John 18:38

And he said unto them the third time, why, what evil hath he done? I have found no cause of death in him: I will therefore chastise him, and let him go. Luke 23:22

But when that final attempt to deliver Jesus from the Jews also failed, then *he delivered him to be crucified.*

The Will of the People Demanded the Death Penalty

The Jewish rulers and people made their case:

And they were instant with loud voices, requiring that he might be crucified. And the voices of them and of the chief priests prevailed. Luke 23:23

Even though Darius had worked to spare Daniel, the Chaldean parliament prevailed; on the basis of the existing law, Daniel must die.

Then these men assembled unto the king, and said unto the king, Know, O king, that the law of the Medes and Persians is, That no decree nor statute which the king establisheth may be changed. Dan. 6:15

Ruler Trapped by the Law

And Pilate gave sentence that it should be as they required.
Luke 23:24

Pilate was trapped by the pressure of the people and the existing laws and customs,

And so Pilate, willing to content the people, released Barabbas unto them, and delivered Jesus, when he had scourged him, to be crucified. Mark 15:15

Likewise, ensnared by his own law, King Darius bowed to the wishes of the people:

Then the king commanded, and they brought Daniel, and cast him into the den of lions. Dan. 6:16a

Gentile Ruler Spoke Prophetically

[Pilate]...*saith unto the Jews, Behold your King!*
John 19:14

And...[wrote]...*THIS IS JESUS THE KING OF THE JEWS.*
Mat. 27:37

Darius speaking by revelation made a statement of great faith.

Now the king spake and said unto Daniel, Thy god whom thou servest continually, he will deliver thee. Dan. 6:16b

Jesus Placed in a Manmade Cave (Tomb)
Burial Place for the Dead

The bodies of both men were placed by other men in a cave hollowed out of rock by man.

World Expected Jesus to Remain in Tomb

The tomb and den were places where death was the norm and where the bodies of Jesus and Daniel were expected to remain until consumed.

Tomb of Jesus Sealed with a Stone

Pilate said unto them, Ye have a watch: go your way, make it as sure as ye can. So they went, and made the sepulchre sure, sealing the stone, and setting a watch.

Mat. 27:65-66

Jesus' tomb was a cave, its entry blocked with a huge stone, and sealed, and a guard placed about it. It, was a lion's den, because it was the work of the roaring lion, the Devourer, the Enemy of our souls, who sought Jesus' death.

And a stone was brought, and laid upon the mouth of the den. Dan. 6:17a

Tomb of Jesus Sealed with a Seal

And the king sealed it with his own signet, and with the signet of his lords; that the purpose might not be changed concerning Daniel. Dan. 6:17b

The den of the lions was made sure by placing a stone and a seal upon it, so there could be no chance for Daniel's friends to get him out. Perhaps Darius also wished to protect Daniel from his enemies, should Daniel's God somehow manage to protect him from the lions; and avert the death penalty.

Jesus Had Precedents for His Faith

Our fathers trusted in thee: they trusted, and thou didst deliver them. Psa. 22:4

Psalm 22 records that Jesus relied upon God's history of deliverance for strength while on the cross. Daniel was also aware of God's deliverance of his three companions from the fiery furnace, as well as his own life which had been spared by God's revealing wisdom.

Jesus Was under Lion Attack

Psalm 22 echoes with phrases that could have been as easily uttered by Daniel as by Jesus.

Be not far from me; for trouble is near; for there is none to help. (11)
Many bulls have compassed me: strong bulls of Bashan have beset me round. (12)
They gaped upon me with their mouths, as a ravening and a roaring lion. (13)
For dogs [gentiles] *have compassed me: the assembly of the wicked have enclosed me.* (16a)

Deliver my soul from the sword; my darling from the power of the dog. (20)
Save me from the lion's mouth: for thou hast heard me. (21)

"Darling" in verse 20 is literally "beloved," or "only child." Psalm 35:17 is even clearer: "*Lord, how long wilt thou look on? rescue my soul from their destructions, my darling from the lions.*" Psa. 35:17)

In Acts chapter two the Holy Spirit gave His own commentary of the Messiah's resurrection expanding on Psalm 16:10.

David...a prophet...seeing this before spake of the resurrection of Christ, that his soul was not left in hell, neither his flesh did see corruption. Acts 2:29-31

Both Jesus and Daniel were under attack, and their lives in danger due to the presence of the lions, yet Jesus maintained,

I will declare thy name unto my brethren: in the midst of the congregation will I praise thee. (22)
For he hath not despised nor abhorred the affliction of the afflicted; neither hath he hid his face from him; but when he cried unto him, he heard. (24)
All the ends of the world shall remember and turn unto the Lord: and all the kindreds of the nations shall worship before thee. (27)
They shall come, and shall declare his righteousness unto a people that shall be born, that he hath done this. (31)

Verse 31 is still being declared today, and could have been written of either Daniel or Jesus, because these two accounts, of Daniel in the Lion's Den and Jesus Christ upon the Cross, are probably two of the most familiar in all of literature. Even the secular world knows these stories well.

The King of Heaven Did Not Sleep

Jesus' Father in Heaven was keenly aware of the evil trial, and the wicked cross prepared for His beloved Son. He was not a disinterested spectator any more than was Darius.

Behold, he that keepeth Israel shall neither slumber nor sleep. Psa. 121:4b

The earthly King, Darius, did not sleep either:

Then the king went to his palace, and passed the night fasting: neither were instruments of music brought before him: and his sleep went from him. Dan. 6:18

Darius used spiritual disciplines, to act upon faith and his recorded actions are the same as those employed by Paul in the New Testament era:

In labours, in watchings, in fastings. 2 Cor. 6:5b

The King Arrived Early

The king arose very early in the morning, and went in haste unto the den of lions. Dan. 6:19

Both the lions' den and the tomb were sealed: King Darius appeared at the "tomb" of Daniel, probably before sunrise. The Father, the King of Heaven, was also intimately involved in what was taking place at the tomb of Jesus. He also came early to the tomb. However, He was there, not to question, but to act.

Killed the Prince of life, whom God hath raised from the dead. Acts 3:15

Be it known unto you all, and to all the people of Israel, that by the name of Jesus Christ of Nazareth, whom ye crucified, whom God raised from the dead, even by him doth this man stand here before you whole. Acts 4:10

And to wait for his Son from heaven, whom he raised from the dead, even Jesus, which delivered us from the wrath to come. 1 Thes. 1:10

God has promised to always be found by His people when they "seek Him early." Darius was hoping to see His miraculous work early that morning.

I love them that love me; and those that seek me early shall find me. Prov. 8:17

The earthly king came to the place where Daniel's dead body was supposed to be, as a type of the women at Jesus's tomb.

And when he came to the den, he cried with a lamentable voice unto Daniel: and the king spake and said to Daniel, O Daniel, servant of the living God, is thy God, whom thou servest continually, able to deliver thee from the lions?
Dan. 6:20

Darius's words express his respect for Daniel's faithfulness to his God. The world may not agree with us, as they did not agree with Daniel, but they will one day have to acknowledge our faithfulness, if we trust God as Daniel did.

Darius' early morning visit is like Mary's, who also went very early in the morning to the tomb of Jesus, looked into the tomb and cried with a lamentable voice.

The first day of the week cometh Mary Magdalene early, when it was yet dark, unto the sepulchre, and seeth the stone taken away from the sepulchre. But Mary stood without at the sepulchre weeping: and as she wept, she stooped down, and looked into the sepulchre. And they say unto her, Woman, why weepest thou? She saith unto them, Because they have taken away my Lord, and I know not where they have laid him. John 20:1,11,13

Mary was weeping, lamenting, because she wasn't sure what had happened to the One whom she sought. Both she and Darius were seekers at the tomb.

In addition, Darius stands as a symbol of God the Father, who was apparently honor-bound by the decree of His own law (by His own Word) not to interfere, nor approach the place of testing until the period of testing was completed

Jesus's Testifies to Being Raised by the Father

Then said Daniel unto the king, O king, live for ever. My God hath sent his angel, and hath shut the lions' mouths, that they have not hurt me: forasmuch as before him innocency was found in me; and also before thee, O king, have I done no hurt. Dan. 6:21-22

These words spoken by Daniel could have been spoken nearly five hundred years later by the Son of God, summarized as "My God has defeated the enemy's attempted work upon me." Jesus enjoyed that same protection based upon faith and bequeathed it to His followers:

And these signs shall follow them that believe; In my name shall they cast out devils; they shall speak with new tongues; They shall take up serpents; and if they drink any deadly thing, it shall not hurt them; they shall lay hands on the sick, and they shall recover. Mark 16:17-18

Behold, I give unto you power to tread on serpents and scorpions, and over all the power of the enemy: and nothing shall by any means hurt you. Luke 10:19

Jesus Was Innocent

Daniel explained his deliverance by stating that "innocency" was found in him; he had neither wronged God nor man. This was also Jesus's testimony:

For the prince of this world cometh, and hath nothing in me. John 14:30

The Command for Jesus to Be Raised Is Issued

Then was the king exceeding glad for him, and commanded that they should take Daniel up out of the den. So Daniel was taken up out of the den, and no manner of hurt was found upon him, because he believed in his God.

Dan. 6:23

God the Father also issued a command for Jesus to be raised from the dead.

And killed the Prince of life, whom God hath raised from the dead; whereof we are witnesses. Acts 3:15

Paul, an apostle, (not of men, neither by man, but by Jesus Christ, and God the Father, who raised him from the dead;) Gal. 1:1

Ye are risen with him through the faith of the operation of God, who hath raised him from the dead. Col. 2:12

The King's divine commandment preceded Daniel being taken up from the place of death. So it was at Jesus' resurrection from the dead. The Father issued the divine command, and the Spirit of God energized the dead body of Jesus, restoring life to it, a blessing which also awaits each believer.

But if the Spirit of him that raised up Jesus from the dead dwell in you, he that raised up Christ from the dead shall also quicken your mortal bodies by his Spirit that dwelleth in you. Rom. 8:11

Jesus Came out of the Tomb Alive

He is not here: for he is risen, as he said. Mat. 28:6a

And when they found not his body, they came, saying... he was alive. Luke 24:23

To the amazement of others, Daniel and Jesus each came forth alive out of a place of death; one from a lions' den, the other from a tomb.

Permission Granted to Remove the Body

On a lesser level of symbolism, Darius' command for the men to bring Daniel up from the den parallels that of Pilate to Joseph of Arimathea to remove the body of Jesus from the tree, and place it in the tomb. Just as Pilate gave permission to Joseph, so Darius gave permission to Daniel to leave the lions' den.

Faith Is the Basis for Resurrection

Jesus believed in the Word, the promise of God, to Him, as recorded by David,

For thou wilt not leave my soul in hell; neither wilt thou suffer thine Holy One to see corruption. Psa. 16:10

It is our faith in the resurrection of Jesus Christ that assures us of salvation and of our own resurrection.

That if thou shalt confess with thy mouth the Lord Jesus, and shalt believe in thine heart that God hath raised him from the dead, thou shalt be saved. Rom. 10:9

The Holy Spirit revealed Daniel's heart in Daniel 6:23, when He observed that his deliverance came "*because he believed in his God.*"

Finally, my brethren, be strong in the Lord, and in the power of his might. Eph. 6:10

Daniel trusted in God's power to deliver him. Conversely, no power of the enemy was able to destroy Him!

The Betrayer of Jesus Dies Himself

And the king commanded, and they brought those men which had accused Daniel, and they cast them into the den of lions, them, their children, and their wives; and the lions had the mastery of them, and brake all their bones in pieces or ever they came at the bottom of the den. Dan. 6:24

The men who plotted Daniel's death were put to death in the same manner which they intended for Daniel. Judas who assembled men to take Jesus, for his efforts gained death; and the fee for his betrayal bought a potter's field to be used for burying the poor, as Matthew related.

Accuser of Jesus Acquired a Place of Death

Then Judas, which had betrayed him, when he saw that he was condemned, repented himself, and brought again the thirty pieces of silver to the chief priests and elders, Saying, I have sinned in that I have betrayed the innocent blood. And they said, What is that to us? see thou to that. And he cast down the pieces of silver in the temple, and departed, and went and hanged himself. And the chief priests took the silver pieces, and said, It is not lawful for to put them into the treasury, because it is the price of blood. And they took counsel, and bought with them the potter's field, to bury strangers in. Wherefore that field was called, The field of blood, unto this day. Mat. 27:3-8

Those who assembled themselves to betray Daniel also acquired a place of death, a place that would be filled with the broken bones of the dead.

Not a Bone of Him Was Broken

Daniel was preserved like Him of whom it was written,

These things were done, that the scripture should be fulfilled, A bone of him shall not be broken. John 19:36

None of Jesus's bones were broken as was prophesied. This was a fulfillment of another type, Jesus as the Passover Lamb of God:

And the Lord said...this is the ordinance of the Passover ...neither shall ye break a bone thereof. Exo. 12:43-46

None of Daniel's bones were broken either, yet the bones of his enemies, including wives and children, were broken by the lions before their bodies even hit the bottom of the pit. This indicates the ferocity of the lions and the extent of the miracle Daniel experienced.

The last statement of Daniel 6:24 is significant in that *the lions had the mastery of them.* This illustrates the fact that Satan, the roaring lion controls, rules over, has mastery of the haters of God.

God Pronounced Judgment upon Enemies of His Son

Jesus taught about His Father's judgment in the parable of the vineyard:

But when the husbandmen saw the son, they said among themselves, This is the heir; come, let us kill him, and let us seize on his inheritance. And they caught him, and cast him out of the vineyard, and slew him...He will miserably destroy those wicked men, and will let out his vineyard unto other husbandmen. Mat. 21:38,39,41

Darius again represented God the Father as he pronounced judgment upon those who sought to kill Daniel. Darius, like God the Father who proclaimed judgment for those who hated His greater Son, now pronounced sentence, doomed them to the same manner of death which they had intended for Daniel.

A similar experience is recorded in the Book of Esther Haman hated Mordecai. He had an illogical hatred of the Jews and offered money to have them killed.

And he thought scorn to lay hands on Mordecai alone; for they had showed him the people of Mordecai: wherefore Haman sought to destroy all the Jews that were throughout the whole kingdom of Ahasuerus, even the people of Mordecai.
If it please the king, let it be written that they may be destroyed: and I will pay ten thousand talents of silver to the hands of those that have the charge of the business, to bring it into the king's treasuries.
And the letters were sent by posts into all the king's provinces, to destroy, to kill, and to cause to perish, all Jews, both young and old, little children and women, in one day. Est. 3:6,9,13a

And the thing pleased Haman; and he caused the gallows to be made. Est. 5:14b

On that night could not the king sleep, and he commanded to bring the book of records of the chronicles; and they were read before the king. Est. 6:1

Another King, who could not sleep, became the recipient of truth that came in the night. Once again, silver was the medium of exchange for death; the price paid for killing a Jew.

Then the king said, Hang him [Haman] *thereon. So they hanged Haman on the gallows that he had prepared for Mordecai.* Est. 7:9b,10a

It is ironic, yet fitting, that those who attempted to send Daniel to his doom were themselves doomed, sentenced by the very words they had pronounced from their own mouths. They went to the same kind of death, into the jaws of the same lions which they had intended for Daniel. They fell prey to the curse spoken from their own mouths; thus they decreed and brought destruction upon themselves. The Jews of Jesus' day pronounced their own doom:

Then answered ***all the people****, and said, His blood be* ***on us, and on our children****.* Mat. 27:25

In both instances it would appear that the betrayers cursed not only themselves, but also brought a curse upon their children.

Although the parallels between the sentences and deliverances of Daniel and Jesus are beautiful, God's purpose is far greater than mere beauty. Both deliverance produced a decree or covenant offering life. There is an almost unbelievably symbolic and prophetic parallel with the *New Testament*, and the covenant for which it is named.

King Proclaims a New Decree

Darius' decree contains an amazing statement of faith from a gentile king:

Then king Darius wrote unto all people, nations, and languages, that dwell in all the earth; Peace be multiplied unto you.
I make a decree, That in every dominion of my kingdom men tremble and fear before the God of Daniel: for he is ***the living God, and stedfast for ever,*** *and his kingdom that which shall not be destroyed, and his dominion shall be* ***even unto the end****.*
He delivereth and rescueth, and he ***worketh signs and wonders*** *in heaven and in earth, who hath delivered Daniel from the* ***power of the lions.*** Dan. 6:25-27

The God and Father of our Lord Jesus Christ, likewise is *the living God, and stedfast for ever,* and His kingdom and dominion will last to the end of time. In addition, our God continued to work signs and wonders in the New Testament. It is still His will to do so today.

King of Heaven Instituted a New Covenant

King Darius issued a new decree as a result of what God accomplished because of the faith of Daniel in the place of death. The king's new commandment was, in effect, **a new covenant** made for all the people within his kingdom. Our Heavenly Father also made *a New Covenant,* made for all the people within His Kingdom. The King of Heaven issued an edict, a new covenant, as a result of His Son's resurrection from the grave.

Covenant Based on Jesus' Completed Work

The basis for the New Covenant was Jesus' Blood, His completed work upon the Cross, and His resurrection from the dead. King Darius made his new decree as a result of what God did through the working of Daniel's faith in the place of death, facing death in the presence of the lions.

Jesus Offered a Covenant of Life

Having formerly made a law unto death, Darius made a second decree, unto life. He superseded the previous decree with a new covenant of life and peace, as God did through Jesus Christ.

The law...work(s)...to bring forth fruit unto death. Rom. 7:5

For the law of the Spirit of life in Christ Jesus hath made me free from the law of sin and death. Rom. 8:2

Jesus Received a Miracle of Life

A miracle of life was demonstrated in each man's life. God granted life when death should have occurred! Both Daniel and Jesus were raised alive from their places of entombment and exist as testimonies to God's omnipotent power!

Result of Jesus' Miracle Extended to Others

A miracle occurred in the den of lions for Daniel, and for all in the kingdom who would subsequently enjoy as a result of it, the benefits of the King's second decree. A miracle occurred in the tomb of Jesus for Him, and for all who subsequently enjoy the blessed results of the Heavenly King's Covenant.

God's Covenant a Covenant of Peace

And came and preached peace to you which were afar off, and to them that were nigh. Eph. 2:17

The covenant based upon Daniel's completed work in the den, included peace.

Peace be multiplied unto you. Dan. 6:25

All the people under Darius' rule enjoyed
* a covenant of peace; *Peace be multiplied unto you;*
* a covenant based upon reverence for God *men tremble and fear before the God of Daniel for He is the living God*;
* a covenant that commended God's steadfast, faithfulness;
* a covenant that acknowledged the indestructibility and eternal duration of his kingdom; and finally
* a covenant which recognized his Omnipotent power and dominion.

Jesus's Covenant Covered All in His Kingdom

For the promise is unto you, and to your children, and to all that are afar off, even as many as the Lord our God shall call. Acts 2:39

Both covenants were universal covering all those who were in subjection to the kings of the respective kingdoms. Since Darius was a ruler of Babylon which was a one world government, his decree extended to the whole earth, as does God's.

Jesus' Work and God's Covenant Are for All Languages

Thou wast slain, and hast redeemed us to God by thy blood out of every kindred, and tongue, and people, and nation.
Rev. 5:9

Similarly Darius' edict was to all people, nations and languages of the known world. Another gentile king, Pilate wrote a title which could be read in the three recognized languages of the day.

And a superscription also was written over him in letters of Greek, and Latin, and Hebrew, THIS IS THE KING OF THE JEWS.
Luke 23:38

God's Covenant Is a Blood Covenant

The God of Heaven made a *blood* Covenant with His people, for all His subjects, based upon the most precious possible substance, the blood of His own dear Son. It was the most solemn, binding form of agreement possible, backed by His throne, His Word and by the Blood of God!

However, Darius' decree also involved the shedding of blood. It was made after the shedding of far inferior blood, that of enemies, but nevertheless, it points to that greater covenant which it foreshadowed, as did the blood of bulls and goats.

Jesus Prophesied the Good News Would Be Announced to the World Before the End

And this gospel of the kingdom shall be preached in all the world for a witness unto all nations; and then shall the end come. Mat 24:14

Daniel recorded the universal decree of Darius containing good news which was addressed,

Unto all people, nations, and languages, that dwell in all the earth. Dan. 6:25

Covenant Required Reverence for the God of Heaven

Both God's covenant and the decree of Darius exalted and expected reverence for the true God of Heaven.

Jesus Was Silent, Did Not Resist

He was oppressed, and he was afflicted, yet he opened not his mouth: he is brought as a lamb to the slaughter, and as a sheep before her shearers is dumb, so he openeth not his mouth. Isa. 53:7

There is no record that Daniel resisted the unjust sentence pronounced upon him, much like Jesus who,

Being found in fashion as a man, he humbled himself, and became obedient unto death, even the death of the cross.
Phil. 2:8

Jesus after Being Humbled Was Exalted

Because of His perfect and completed work, Jesus was exalted and restored to the position which He occupied formerly with the Father, before He descended into a lower place, the earth, and faced death.

Wherefore God also hath highly exalted him, and given him a name which is above every name. Phil. 2:9

Daniel was likewise restored to the exalted position which he formerly held, and was honored, both by Darius and by his successor in the kingdom which followed.

So this Daniel prospered in the reign of Darius, and in the reign of Cyrus the Persian. Dan. 6:28

Jesus Prospered During the Reign of His Father, and Will Reign in the Millennium

If Darius is an archetype of God the Father, as has been proposed, then the Book of Daniel holds an internal prophecy of the future reign of Jesus Christ during the millennium. He must reign in the millennium as the Scriptures describe, because He has not yet prospered as Daniel did subsequent to his deliverance from the lions.

Cyrus is a foreshadowing of the Messiah. He issued a commandment for Jerusalem to be restored, (See Isaiah's prophecy in the Preface of this chapter) and is thus a type of the Messiah who will restore the Holy City. **So Jesus, like Daniel, will rule in the reign following the present one.**

ADDITIONAL AMAZING PARALLELS

Parallels exist in other chapters of Daniel in addition to those in the sixth chapter, there are a number of other exciting parallels between Daniel and Jesus Christ. Some that I have found follow. You will, no doubt, find others.

Jesus Was the Seed (Offspring) of a King

Jesus was not only heir to the throne of heaven, but also an heir to the throne of David. Thus, the Magi asked,

Where is he that is born King of the Jews? for we...are come to worship him. Mat. 2:2

Bring certain of the children of Israel, and of the king's seed, and of the princes. Dan. 1:3

Since Daniel was in the palace at Jerusalem and was among the "king's seed" and "the princes," he was apparently of noble birth, no doubt a potential heir to the throne. Like Him whom he foreshadowed, Daniel was "born to be king."

Jesus Was Hated Because He Was to Be a King

Satan always hated and feared *king's seed*, because he knew the predictions that Messiah would be of royal seed, and that He would be an heir of David's throne. After Jesus' birth, Herod attempted to kill all young males who might be *He that is born King of the Jews.* (Mat. 2:2a) Similarly in Daniel's day, Nebuchadnezzar, no doubt, hated and feared a potential Jewish King and so either killed or took captive all the young men who might later have become a ruler in Jerusalem. (1:3)

Jesus Forced to Leave Judah

In His youth, Jesus was forced to flee from Judah when Joseph was warned in a dream by God to do so. Likewise, Daniel was forced to leave Judah, the land of his nativity in captivity, or he would have been killed.

Jesus Carried to Gentile Nation to Save His Life

Jesus was carried away by His family to Egypt to protect His life. As a young man, Daniel was spared from death when he was carried off to Shinar with the other treasures of the Temple. Both were carried to a gentile nation, an act which saved their lives.

Jesus Was a Lamb Without Blemish

Jesus, as the Passover Lamb of God, had to be a male without spot or blemish.

Your lamb shall be without blemish. Exo. 12:5

Pilate...saith unto them, Behold, I bring him forth to you, that ye may know that I find no fault in him. John 19:4

Daniel, like Jesus, was without blemish.

In whom was no blemish. Dan. 1:4

Jesus Knew How to Pray

One of his disciples said unto him, Lord, teach us to pray.
Luke 11:1

Daniel was also considered successful in praying to get results and the best in the kingdom at receiving answers from heaven.

Jesus Increased in Wisdom

And Jesus increased in wisdom. Luke 2:52

Daniel was also filled with wisdom and the wisdom which he was granted increased. At the beginning of his career in Babylon it was tested and found to have become tenfold greater than that of the wisest competition.

Jesus Increased in Favor

And Jesus increased...in favor with God and man.
Luke 2:52

Now God had brought Daniel into favour and tender love with the prince of the eunuchs. Dan. 1:9

Jesus Slept During a Life-Threatening Storm

And he was in...the ship, asleep on a pillow: and they awake him, and say...Master, carest thou not that we perish? Mark 4:38

Consider that Daniel apparently went to bed and slept in faith and trust, although under threat of death, after he and his friends made their request to God for an answer in Daniel chapter two. He, too, slept in a life-threatening storm. Daniel went to bed in faith, believing that God would answer. His action presupposes a knowledge of God's goodness, a satisfaction that His word is true and that He is true to His Word! It also indicates his knowledge that God will not abandon His children when they are in need.

Leaders Sought to Kill Jesus and Friends

And consulted that they might take Jesus...and kill him.
Mat. 26:4

Because the Jews sought to kill him...I am he...let these go their way. John 7:1; 18:8

Daniel and his three companions were similarly sought for the same end.

They sought Daniel and his fellows to be slain. Dan. 2:13

Jesus Sought Prayer in Agreement for Others

Jesus sought joint prayer support for the potential sheep of His flock.

Then saith he unto his disciples...the labourers are few; Pray ye therefore the Lord of the harvest, that he will send forth labourers.[12] Mat. 9:37-38

Daniel sought prayer in agreement with his three friends for the lives of all the wise men to be spared.

Daniel made the thing known to...his companions: That they would desire mercies of the God of heaven concerning this secret. Dan. 2:18

Jesus Regularly Received Revelation

Jesus evidenced supernatural knowledge and wisdom regularly, as at the healing of the palsied man, the healing of the woman with the flow of blood, and concerning His own future:

And Jesus knowing their thoughts. Mat. 9:4
And Jesus, immediately knowing in himself that virtue had gone out of him. Mark 5:30
There appeared...Moses and Elias talking with him. Mat. 17:3

Daniel regularly received secrets of wisdom from God through dreams, visions, revelations and visitations.

Then was the secret revealed unto Daniel. Dan. 2:19

Jesus Gave God the Glory for His Actions

Jesus acknowledged God as the source of all that He did.

[12] A revelation concerning how the Lord Jesus Christ provided for the answering of this prayer is contained in the book *Three Kinds of Faith*.

The words that I speak unto you I speak not of myself: but the Father that dwelleth in me, he doeth the works.
John 14:10

Daniel gave God the glory.

He [God] *revealeth the deep and secret things.*
Dan. 2:22

Jesus Was Filled with Wisdom By God

And the child grew, and waxed strong in spirit, filled with wisdom. Luke 2:40

We have seen that God also filled Daniel with wisdom to the amazement of his fellow man.

I have even heard of thee...that light and understanding and excellent wisdom is found in thee. Dan. 5:14

Jesus Read Supernatural Writing

As the finger of God had in the past written God's convicting words upon tablets of stone, Jesus wrote with the finger of God upon the ground and apparently received a message of wisdom to escape the snare the Pharisees laid for Him.

Jesus stooped down, and with his finger wrote on the ground...when they continued asking him, he...said unto them, He that is without sin among you, let him first cast a stone. John 8:6-7

Daniel also read a message written by the finger of God upon the plaster of Belshazzar's palace wall.

Then Daniel...said...I will read the writing and make known the interpretation. Dan. 5:17

Jesus Expressed His Gratitude to God.

Jesus often gave thanks to His Father as at the raising of Lazarus (John 11:41b), and for freely granting wisdom.

At that time Jesus answered and said, I thank thee, O Father, Lord of heaven and earth, because thou hast hid these things from the wise and prudent, and hast revealed them unto babes. Mat. 11:25

Daniel likewise often gave thanks before His God as he did, in the sixth chapter when his life was threatened.

Now...Daniel...prayed, and gave thanks before his God, as he did aforetime. Dan. 6:10

Jesus Was a Prophet

As God promised to Moses, Jesus was a prophet of God similar to Moses.

I will raise them up a Prophet from among their brethren, like unto thee, and will put my words in his mouth; and he shall speak unto them all that I shall command him.
Deut. 18:18

Daniel, of course, was a prophet, and the author of one of the most prophetic books of the Bible.

Jesus Promised Power for God's People

He that believeth on me, the works that I do shall he do also; and greater works than these shall he do; because I go unto my Father. John 14:12

Daniel relayed a similar promise:

The people that do know their God shall be strong, and do exploits. Dan. 11:32

Jesus Spoke of the End of Time

So shall it be in the end of this world. Mat. 13:40

Daniel wrote of the same time period.

Know what shall be in the last end of the indignation: for at the time appointed the end shall be. Dan. 8:19

Jesus Foretold His Supernatural Death

Began Jesus to show...he must...suffer many things... and be killed, and be raised again the third day. Mat. 16:21

Daniel also foretold Jesus' sacrificial death which would be for the benefit of others.

And after threescore and two weeks shall Messiah be cut off, but not for himself. Dan. 9:26

Jesus Promised to Come Again

I will come again, and receive you unto myself; that where I am, there ye may be also. John 14:3

Daniel gave the timing for the Messiah's return.

Know...that from the going forth of the commandment to restore and to build Jerusalem unto the Messiah the Prince shall be seven weeks, and threescore and two weeks. Dan. 9:25

Jesus Predicted Destruction of Temple

And Jesus went out...and his disciples came to him...to show him the buildings of the temple. And Jesus said...verily I say unto you, There shall not be left here one stone upon another, that shall not be thrown down. Mat. 1-2

So did Daniel.

Yea...the daily sacrifice was taken away, and the place of his sanctuary was cast down. Dan 8:11

Jesus Predicted the Overthrow of Jerusalem

O Jerusalem, Jerusalem, thou that killest the prophets, and stonest them which are sent unto thee...Behold, your house is left unto you desolate. Mat. 23:37-38

There shall not be left...one stone upon another, that shall not be thrown down. Mat. 24:2

Daniel described the dual destruction of the city and temple by the people of the coming ruler.

The people of the prince that shall come shall destroy the city and the sanctuary. Dan. 9:26

Jesus Prophesied Gentiles Would Control Jerusalem

And they shall fall by the edge of the sword, and shall be led away captive into all nations: and Jerusalem shall be trodden down of the Gentiles, until the times of the Gentiles be fulfilled. Luke 21:24

Daniel received the same revelation more than five hundred and fifty years earlier.

And they that understand among the people shall instruct many: yet they shall fall by the sword, and by flame, by captivity, and by spoil, many days. Dan. 11:33

How long shall be the vision concerning the daily sacrifice, and the transgression of desolation, to give both the sanctuary and the host to be trodden under foot?
Dan 8:13

Jerusalem's Destruction Was a Result of Rejecting One Sent by God

Jesus gave a warning earlier in His ministry and gave the reason for Jerusalem's coming judgement...

And when he was come near, he beheld the city, and wept over it, Saying, If thou hadst known, even thou, at least in this thy day, the things which belong unto thy peace! but now they are hid from thine eyes. For the days shall come upon thee, that thine enemies shall cast a trench about thee, and compass thee round, and keep thee in on every side, And shall lay thee even with the ground, and thy children within thee; and they shall not leave in thee one stone upon another; because thou knewest not the time of thy visitation. Luke 19:41-44

Judgment would fall upon them for rejecting their King. The Father loved both the City and the occupants. He would have spared them but they rejected His loving offer. *Jesus wept* over the city, because it (in the person of its occupants) rejected Him, and thus decreed its own destruction, because they ignored their King's offer of Himself.

Daniel had almost the exact same warning and understanding upon his heart.

I Daniel understood... the desolations of Jerusalem. We have...rebelled, even by departing from thy precepts and from thy judgments: Neither have we hearkened unto thy servants the prophets. Dan. 9:2,5-6

Jesus Was Asked When the End Would Come

And as he sat upon the mount of Olives, the disciples came unto him privately, saying, Tell us, when shall these things be? Mat. 24:3

Daniel presented almost the identical question.

How long shall it be to the end of these wonders?
Dan. 12:6

Jesus Warned Many Believers Would Perish

For then shall be great tribulation...And except those days should be shortened, there should no flesh be saved: but for the elect's sake those days shall be shortened.
Mat. 24:21,22

A similar ominous theme echoed in Daniel's writing.

And they that understand among the people shall instruct many: yet they shall fall by the sword, and by flame, by captivity, and by spoil, many days. Dan. 11:33

Jesus Will Be upon a Throne

And before him shall be gathered all nations: and he shall separate them one from another, as a shepherd divideth his sheep from the goats. Mat. 25:32

Daniel described His throne.

I beheld...the Ancient of days did sit...his throne was like the fiery flame. Dan. 7:9

Jesus Has an Everlasting Kingdom

He shall be...called the Son of the Highest: and the Lord God shall give unto him the throne of his father David:

And he shall reign over the house of Jacob for ever; and of his kingdom there shall be no end. Luke 1:32-33

Daniel saw this in advance.

I saw in the night visions, and, behold, one like the Son of man...was given...dominion, and glory, and a kingdom, that all people, nations, and languages, should serve him: his dominion is an everlasting dominion, which shall not pass away, and his kingdom that which shall not be destroyed. Dan 7:13-14

The same theme of redemption out of all nations, and of rule with Him, is echoed in Revelation.

And they sung a new song, saying, Thou art worthy to take the book, and to open the seals thereof: for thou wast slain, and hast redeemed us to God by thy blood out of every kindred, and tongue, and people, and nation; And hast made us unto our God kings and priests: and we shall reign on the earth. Rev. 5:9-10

Jesus' Followers to Inherit Kingdom

Come, ye blessed...inherit the kingdom prepared for you from the foundation of the world. Mat. 25:34

Daniel predicted the same bestowal upon the believers:

And the kingdom...shall be given to the people of the saints of the most High, whose kingdom is an everlasting kingdom. Dan. 7:27

Jesus Promised Kingdom Will Be Possessed by Believers

Fear not, little flock; for it is your Father's good pleasure to give you the kingdom. Luke 12:32

A man child, who was to rule all nations with a rod of iron: and her child was caught up unto God, and to his throne. Rev. 12:5

Daniel presented the same thought.

Until the Ancient of days came...and the time came that the saints possessed the kingdom. Dan. 7:22

Jesus Warned of the Abomination of Desolation

When ye therefore shall see the abomination of desolation, spoken of by Daniel the prophet, stand in the holy place, (whoso readeth, let him understand:) Mat. 24:15

Daniel observed the same.

The daily sacrifice shall be taken away, and the abomination that maketh desolate set up. Dan. 12:11

Jesus Identified the Liar, the Enemy of the Truth

Your father the devil...abode not in the truth, because there is no truth in him. When he speaketh a lie, he speaketh of his own: for he is a liar, and the father of it. John 8:44

Daniel also described one who would,

Cast down the truth to the ground. Dan. 8:12

Jesus Predicted "Great Tribulation"

For then shall be great tribulation, such as was not since the beginning of the world. Mat. 24:21

Daniel also wrote of a time of such trouble, as had never before existed.

There shall be a time of trouble, such as never was since there was a nation. Dan. 12:1

Jesus' Garments Became White as Snow

Jesus...was transfigured before them. And his raiment became shining, exceeding ***white as snow.*** Mark 9:2-3

Daniel saw One wearing the same kind of garment.
I beheld till... the Ancient of days did sit, whose garment was white as snow. Dan. 7:9

Jesus Promised to Return in the Clouds

And then shall they see the Son of man coming in a cloud with power and great glory. Luke 21:27

Daniel saw Him in a night vision.

Behold, one like the Son of man came with the clouds of heaven. Dan. 7:13

Jesus Cleansed the Temple

And found in the temple those that sold oxen and sheep and doves, and the changers of money sitting: And when he had made a scourge of small cords, he drove them all out of the temple, And said unto them...make not my Father's house an house of merchandise. John 2:16

Daniel predicted a cleansing of the temple.

And...then shall the sanctuary be cleansed. Dan. 8:14

Sound of Jesus' Voice Caused Men to Fall to the Ground

As soon then as he had said unto them, I am he, they went backward, and fell to the ground. John 18:6

Each time Jesus appeared to him, Daniel fell to the ground in a trance as he did in chapter eight.

And I heard a man's voice...which...said, Gabriel, make this man to understand the vision. Now as he was speaking with me, I was in a deep sleep on my face toward the ground. Dan. 8:16,18

Jesus Engaged in the King's Business

Wist [knew] *ye not that I must be about my Father's* [i.e., the King of Heaven's] *business?* Luke 2:49

Daniel served His heavenly Father obediently and with first devotion, but also worked for the earthly king.

And I Daniel...rose up, and did the king's business. Dan. 8:27

Jesus Warned of Sins Against the Father

But if ye forgive not men their trespasses, neither will your Father forgive your trespasses. Mat. 6:15

I have sinned against heaven. Luke 15:18

Daniel too, warned of the consequences of such trespasses.

O Lord...unto us confusion of faces...because of their trespass...trespassed against thee. Dan. 9:7

Jesus Made a Lengthy Fast

And when he had fasted forty days and forty nights, he was afterward an hungered. Mat. 4:2

Daniel practiced fasting, at least partially, and did so regularly. Scripture records two significant fasts, one lasting ten and one twenty-one days.

I ate no pleasant bread, came neither flesh nor wine in my mouth...till three whole weeks were fulfilled. Dan. 10:3

Jesus' Goals Resisted
By Satan and by Demonic Princes

Satan tempted Jesus in the wilderness at the beginning of His ministry, and repeatedly attempted to thwart His work and to cause His death. The angelic messenger told Daniel the delay in answering his twenty-one-day fast and request was due to demonic interference.

Fear not, Daniel...I am come for thy words. But the prince of the kingdom of Persia withstood me one and twenty days. Dan. 10:13

Jesus Taught of Resurrection of the Dead

And shall come forth; they that have done good, unto the resurrection of life; and they that have done evil, unto the resurrection of damnation. John 5:29

Amazingly, Daniel likewise saw resurrection for both the just and the unjust.

And many of them that sleep in the dust of the earth shall awake, some to everlasting life, and some to shame and everlasting contempt. Dan. 12:2

Jesus Promised Eternal Life

And in the world to come life everlasting Luke 18:30

Daniel wrote a promise of eternal life.

And...of them that sleep...shall awake, some to everlasting life. Dan. 12:2

Jesus Promised Some Would Walk with Him in White

A few...shall walk with me in white: for they are worthy. He that overcometh, the same shall be clothed in white raiment...buy of me...white raiment, that thou mayest be clothed, and that the shame of thy nakedness do not appear. Rev. 3:4-5,18

Their robes will be washed in His blood and thereby made white. (Rev. 7:14) Daniel also wrote of martyrdom for some of the righteous

And some of them of understanding shall fall, to try them, and to purge, and to make them white. Dan. 11:35

Jesus Warned of Wars Before the End

And when ye shall hear of wars and rumours of wars...but the end shall not be yet. Mark 13:7

Daniel noted that these were but a prelude to the end, and not the end.

And he shall stir up his power...against the king of the south with a great army; and...the king of the south shall be

stirred up to battle with a very great and mighty army...and many shall fall down slain...but it shall not prosper: for yet the end shall be at the time appointed. Dan. 11:25-27

Jesus Promised a Regathering from the Four Winds

See the Son of Man coming...and...his angels shall gather together his elect from the four winds, from one end of heaven to the other. Mat. 24:30-31

While Jesus predicted the restoration of His Body, Daniel described an earlier division of a kingdom toward the four winds.

Kingdom shall be broken, and shall be divided toward the four winds of heaven. Dan. 11:4

Jesus Warns of the Beast

Jesus made known to John in Revelation, that there would be one symbolically represented as a "beast" who would attack His people.

And it was given unto him to make war with the saints, and to overcome them: and power was given him over all kindreds, and tongues, and nations. Rev. 13:7

Daniel wrote of a similar "horn" which waged war against the saints, and which overpowered them for a season.

I beheld, and the same horn made war with the saints, and prevailed against them. Dan. 7:21

Jesus Promised Blessing for Overcomers

Jesus left us with hope for the future, and upbeat messages for overcomers.

He that endureth to the end shall be saved. Mat 10:22b

The Lamb shall overcome...and they that are with him are [the] *called, and chosen, and faithful.* Rev 17:14

Ye have overcome the wicked one. 1 John 2:13

Daniel closes his book by recording a similar message which he heard from heaven.

Go thy way, Daniel...till the time of the end. Blessed is he that waiteth, and cometh to the...end...for thou shalt rest, and stand...at the end of the days. Dan 12:9,12,13

I am truly awed as I reflect upon the more than one-hundred parallels we have been allowed to see between Daniel and Jesus Christ. The sheer number of them is overpowering. God obviously has a message to convey, intended to underscore His truth for the faithful!

Only the mind of God could have arranged all these prophetic occurrences so perfectly, and at least *five hundred years in advance* of the Messiah's fulfillment of them. What a mighty God we serve!

I trust that your appetite, like mine, has been whetted afresh, to seek God for more of His wisdom, and for more mysteries to be revealed...

CHAPTER TEN

SHARING THE LIGHT

Early one morning vacationing in Florida, I stood on a balcony overlooking the beach. There I saw a small boy about three years old with a plastic pail and bucket. My heart was filled with a surprising warmth of affection, and I felt a great love for that little boy as I watched him trying to put the ocean into the hole which he had dug in the sand. I saw in him my own sons as they played in the sand many years earlier. I was allowed to experience just for a moment a taste of the love of God, of His surprisingly great love for all the sons of God in whom He has been able to see vestiges of His own Beloved Son. His Son was also for a season a child and bore the image of just such a "son of man."

For a moment I felt something of the great compassion that God feels for mankind, as I found myself experiencing love for that child. My love for him, I realized was purely grace, unmerited favor. The child had not done, nor would he probably ever do, anything for me, yet his innocence was pleasing to me. I was struck by the thought of how God loves us in spite of the foolishness of so much that we do, which we take so seriously, just as this boy was seriously trying to move the ocean into his hole.

My prayer again for each reader is that you might be caused to hunger for the deeper things of God, and that you might be stimulated to employ the keys and techniques which have been offered to acquire the wisdom of God.

The Goal of Believers

Our goal is not knowledge for knowledge's sake nor exaltation of self, those are the fruit of the tree of knowledge, but rather to be able to better know, honor, and obey Him whom we seek and serve.

Our heart's desire in seeking wisdom is to glorify God. One can only glorify God by seeking Him, and by receiving from Him. Peter didn't want the Lord to wash his feet, and said, *Thou shalt never wash my feet. Jesus answered him, If I wash thee not, thou hast no part with me.* (John 13:8)

I believe one must receive from God before he can have a testimony to share with others, whether of forgiveness, cleansing, healing, deliverance, or a revelation. Peter had to first receive ministry from the Lord in order to have a part in Jesus' ministry, before he could minister to others, before he could in turn *comfort them which are in any trouble, by the comfort wherewith we ourselves are comforted of God.* (2 Cor. 1:4)

To be able to minister one must first have received something from Jesus. The blind beggar (John 9:8) gave God no glory while begging. However, God got glory when He was healed! After he was healed even the Pharisees demanded that he give God the praise, although they had shown no interest in him previously. Likewise, the Gadarene demoniac had no ministry until after he received deliverance; then Jesus commissioned him,

Go home to thy friends, and tell them how great things the Lord hath done for thee, and hath had compassion on thee.

Mark 5:19

The purpose of this search for wisdom is to be able to live a life that is pleasing to God; in the process we will also get to better know our God and become more like Him.

As you commune with Him, you will find that there is an increasing manifestation of the life of Christ in you. In a normal healthy relationship a son who is proud of his father will seek to emulate his father. So will we seek to become like our Father.

Listen for the voice of Wisdom because

Happy is the man that findeth wisdom, and the man that getteth understanding. My son, let not them depart from thine eyes: keep sound wisdom and discretion: So shall they be life unto thy soul, and grace to thy neck.

Prov. 3:22

Blessed is the man that heareth me, watching daily at my gates, waiting at the posts of my doors. For whoso findeth me findeth life, and shall obtain favour of the Lord.

Prov. 8:35

God's ultimate plan and purpose is to populate the earth with carbon copies of His own dear Son. Even after Adam's fall from obedience, God's continuing desire is for man to be an outworking of His nature, image and Son.

Let us hear the conclusion of the whole matter: Fear God, and keep his commandments: for this is the whole duty of man. Eccl. 12:13

God, the Holy Ghost, can bring these truths into our hearts that we might live in the fullness of His purposes. As we have seen one of the main goals of the Holy Spirit is to enable us to walk in obedience to God, and that we might become like Him, might become Holy.

Jesus stated the goal of God as,

Thou shalt love the Lord thy God with all thy heart, and with all thy soul, and with all thy strength, and with all thy mind; and thy neighbour as thyself. Luke 10:27

He also encouraged us to continue hungering after God, after the True Bread of Heaven, and to keep pressing into the Kingdom of God. Remember your first deep burning love for God? Even if it has been allowed to grow cold, it is always possible to fan the embers and to return to God, as Jesus urged.

Nevertheless I have somewhat against thee, because thou hast left thy first love. Remember therefore from whence thou art fallen, and repent, and do the first works.
Rev. 2:4-5a

A Promised Fullness of Knowledge of the Lord

Isaiah prophesied of a coming day when,

They shall not hurt nor destroy in all my holy mountain: for the earth shall be full of the knowledge of the Lord, as the waters cover the sea. Isa. 11:9

Habakkuk received a similar word, that men should no longer commit bloody acts.

For the earth shall be filled with the knowledge of the glory of the Lord, as the waters cover the sea. Hab. 2:14

Throughout the gospels the voice of Jesus repeatedly tells us, *I will come again.* The Book of Revelation contains the phrase three times, *Behold, I come quickly.*

Our hearts now renewed to think in harmony with the Holy Spirit, join with Him in a joyful response to that glorious promise and cry in unison, *Amen. Even so, come, Lord Jesus.*

APPENDIX

The Whole Armor of God

A Revelation Illustrating the Centrality of Jesus Christ

The intuitive recognition that Jesus is the object of our search and that God's underlying purpose is to reveal Him, helped me even before I fully grasped those principles. More than twenty years ago the Lord gave me a revelation concerning the whole armor of God which illustrates them: the whole armor equals Jesus!

Early in 1972 the Lord gave me an understanding concerning the whole armor of God described in chapter six of Ephesians. More than a dozen years later He showed me another confirmation of that truth and a specific Scriptural statement of its accuracy.

Finally, my brethren, be strong in the Lord, and in the power of His might.
Put on the whole armour of God, that ye may be able to stand against the wiles of the devil.
For we wrestle not against principalities, against powers, against the rulers of the darkness of this world, against spiritual wickedness in high places.
Wherefore take unto you the whole armour of God, that ye may be able to withstand in the evil day, and having done all, to stand.
Stand therefore, having your loins girt about with truth, and having on the breastplate of righteousness;
And your feet shod with the preparation of the gospel of

peace;
Above all, taking the shield of faith, wherewith ye shall be able to quench all the fiery darts of the wicked.
And take the helmet of salvation, and the sword of the Spirit, which is the word of God:
Praying always with all prayer and supplication in the Spirit. Eph. 6:10-18

What is the whole armor of God? A series of questions regarding each element reveals the answer.

Stand therefore having your loins girt about with truth. Who said, *I am the way, the truth, and the life*?

And having on the breastplate of righteousness; Who is the source of our righteousness? Who is the Righteousness of God?

And your feet shod with the preparation of the gospel of peace; Who is the Prince of Peace? In celebration of whose birth did the angels sing, "Peace on earth!"?

Above all, taking the shield of faith, wherewith ye shall be able to quench all the fiery darts of the wicked. Who is it who is the Author and Finisher of our faith?

And take the helmet of salvation, Who is the source of our salvation? Whose very name, *Yeshua*, means salvation?

And the sword of the Spirit, which is the word of God: Who is known as the *Word of God* and also the *Word made flesh*? Who is the very *Logos* of God?

Praying always with all prayer and supplication in the

Spirit, Who it that baptizes us with the Holy Spirit and thereby enables us to *pray in the Spirit*?

Jesus Christ is every element of the armor, and therefore, is Himself the whole armor of God; the very fullness of the Godhead, being all-in-all. He is our Leader, Captain, King, and even our armor; our source of protection. As *Jehovah-Jireh* He provides for our every need, even our protection against the wiles and weapons of our malignant enemy.

Jesus has given us other spiritual equipment, the legal right to another weapon, His Name, before which every knee must ultimately bow. He has also given us power! There are two different words in the Greek of the New Testament which are translated power. Jesus has provided us with both forms: *exousia* is the legal right, or the authority to act; *dunamis* is the dynamite enabling power to do "greater works" than He did because He won the right to pour forth the Spirit upon all willing flesh!

The Lord confirmed the validity of this revelation more than a dozen years later by quickening to me Romans 13:12,14:

The night is far spent, the day is at hand: let us therefore cast off the works of darkness, and let us put on the armour of light.
But put ye on the Lord Jesus Christ and make not provision for the flesh, to fulfill the lusts thereof.

We must dispel the works of darkness, the works of Satan's kingdom, by bringing the light of the Word of God, the light of Jesus, by the illumination of His Holy Spirit, to bear upon them. Rather than being a party to those works of darkness, we must separate ourselves from them and defend ourselves with the armor of light, by *putting on the Lord Jesus Christ*! To **put on Jesus Christ is to put on the whole armor of God!**

As beautiful as this is, God has even more depths of truth in this regard. Any truth about Jesus can be substituted into the formula to represent the elements of the armor.

As long as I am in the world, I am the light of the world.
John 9:5

Jesus is "the Light of the world," and "the armor of light." Jesus is also the "Word of God." Therefore we can correctly say that the Word of God is defensive truth, and provides righteousness, peace, faith, salvation and is properly called the Sword of the Spirit, the Word of God.

GOD'S WISDOM IS DIFFERENT

How Does God's Guidance Come?

If the church hadn't strayed so far from the truth of God there would be no need for the type of teaching in this book. But we have become so influenced by the world, that most believers don't expect to hear God speak.

The Pentecostals once had a tradition of "praying through," of "storming the gates of heaven," until they received an answer. Regrettably, we rarely hear of that today.

Most men don't trust the guidance they get if they do get it, because they have been taught God doesn't speak to men anymore. Millions more don't even expect to hear, and therefore aren't listening. They turn a willfully deaf ear to God.

Elijah provided an important lesson in guidance; he had an enlightening experience hearing the Lord's voice. God directed him,

Go forth, and stand upon the mount before the Lord. And, behold, the Lord passed by, and a great and strong wind rent the mountains, and brake in pieces the rocks before the Lord; but the Lord was not in the wind: and after the wind an earthquake; but the Lord was not in the earthquake:

And after the earthquake a fire; but the Lord was not in the fire: and after the fire ***a still small voice.***

1 Kings 19:11-12

The Lord most commonly speaks to us, I believe, in the still, small, often "inner" voice of the heart. I most frequently simply have a feeling, inwardly and very gently, that I should witness to someone, or pray for someone's healing. There is rarely ever any pressure to the feeling, unless it is something that I already *know* that I am supposed to do, and am resisting. For example, an impression that I should witness to someone, with whom I feel uncomfortable, or where a situation of peer pressure is causing resistance to obedience.

Much of divine guidance is missed because it comes simply as such very gentle nudging in one's spirit. Sometimes He speaks audibly as He apparently did in Acts 13:2, but most often it is less obvious. Usually it comes simply as a persistent inner conviction, which is the gentle wooing by the Holy Spirit to do His will.

First the gentle nudging of the Holy Spirit is experienced *within your spirit*, which is why it is so gentle. Then that nudge may be verbalized into your consciousness either as a realization or as a sudden, yet gentle, awareness that God wants you to do something. Even more often it simply is a feeling that *I should* or *I ought* to do this or that. I may even find myself expressing this to myself, in words such as, "I feel I should witness to that person," or "It seems as if God wants me to go visit that brother."

When *I feel* I should witness to someone, God is communicating by His Spirit to my *spirit*; my spirit then communicates the impression of what it has received into my *soul*; which in turn expresses that impression into action by directing my *body* to do something about it.

The gentle “nudge of God” initially received by me in my spirit is then passed on to my soul, accepted or rejected, and then expressed in my actions (by my body). [This is the proper way God communicates: His Spirit to your spirit, your spirit to your soul and finally your soul to your body. The occult differs in that it seeks to transmit information to your soul (mind, will, intellect), for example, through mental telepathy, extra sensory perception or clairvoyance.

I will instruct thee and teach thee in the way which thou shalt go: I will guide thee with mine eye. Psa. 32:8

With a little reflection, we can readily grasp the imagery of this passage: God will guide us with only a look. I recall how my own father could melt me with just a look. He could, without needing to speak a word, communicate approval and satisfaction or displeasure with just an approving glance or a reproving look.

Human Wisdom

Where is the wise? where is the scribe? where is the disputer of this world? hath not God made foolish the wisdom of this world? 1 Cor. 1:20

The wisdom of the world is in stark contrast to the wisdom of God. Wisdom is either God given and God-honoring, or it is in opposition to God. The wisdom of the world (science falsely so called) is fruitless, unproductive at best and foolish, or demonic at worst.

As soon as human wisdom entered the world, man became estranged from his God. The acquisition of human wisdom exalts self, and promotes rebellious independence.

For the wisdom of this world is foolishness with God.
1 Cor.3:19a

And my speech and my preaching was not with enticing words of man's wisdom, but in demonstration of the Spirit and of power. 1 Cor.2:4

Now we have received, not the spirit of the world, but the spirit which is of God; that we might know the things that are freely given to us of God. Which things also we speak, not in the words which man's wisdom teacheth, but which the Holy Ghost teacheth; comparing spiritual things with spiritual. But the natural man receiveth not the things of the Spirit of God: for they are foolishness unto him: neither can he know them, because they are spiritually discerned.
1 Cor. 2:12-14

Man's wisdom and the wisdom of God stand in stark contrast.

For my thoughts are not your thoughts, neither are your ways my ways, saith the Lord. For as the heavens are higher than the earth, so are my ways higher than your ways, and my thoughts than your thoughts.
Isa. 55:8-9

But the wisdom that is from above is first pure, then peaceable, gentle, and easy to be entreated, full of mercy and good fruits, without partiality, and without hypocrisy.
James 3:17

God's wisdom is as far from human reasoning and earthly wisdom as heaven is from the earth. The mind of fallen man was not designed to accommodate such wisdom or thoughts. Thus, man's mind must be regenerated just as his spirit and soul must be. Man requires a "renewed" mind if he is to become a receptacle for God's thoughts and to have the capacity to grasp what God wishes to communicate to him.

This will necessitate "putting off the old man," his ways his thoughts, *And be*(ing) *renewed in the spirit of your mind,* (Eph. 4:23) which literally should read, "be renewed **by the Spirit** in your mind." We cannot renew our own minds any more than we can regenerate, or save ourselves, although we can take steps in that direction by seeking God.

Man's wisdom is flawed because it is based upon observations and experiences, which are neither immutable nor infallible. God's wisdom is absolute, complete, eternal and unchanging.

Man really cannot trust in God (have faith in God) as long as he believes that he can "do it himself," can "get along without God," or thinks he can "make it on his own." Paul recognized this truth and personally ceased relying upon his own wisdom and education even though both were extensive. Hear his own testimony:

Though I might also have confidence in the flesh. If any other man thinketh that he hath whereof he might trust in the flesh, I more: Phil. 3:4

I am verily a man which am a Jew, born in Tarsus, a city in Cilicia, yet brought up in this city at the feet of Gamaliel, and taught according to the perfect manner of the law of the fathers, and was zealous toward God, as ye all are this day. Acts 22:3

Yea doubtless, and I count all things but loss for the excellency of ***the knowledge of Christ Jesus my Lord****: for whom I have suffered the loss of all things, and do count them but dung, that I may win Christ.* Phil. 3:8

Paul valued his knowledge of Christ more highly than all his own impressive credentials, of which he determined not to boast. It wasn't until Paul put aside all of his trust in himself that he could fully put his trust in Jesus Christ, that Christ could become his all sufficiency.

Forbidden Sources of Wisdom, Secret Knowledge

Closely related to human wisdom and the wisdom of this world, is that wisdom which has infiltrated both, and has its source in the occult.

Satan's allure from the beginning has always been a shortcut to by-pass God, a quick, easy way to know the future, to obtain hidden wisdom, or secret knowledge, by sidestepping God's designated, or chosen paths. God forbids the whole occult realm including the Satanic counterfeits of prophecy or the imparting of that which is supposed to be the hidden wisdom of God, such as fortune tellers, Ouija Boards, reading of tea leaves, divination, horoscopes, and all other secret or hidden wisdom, as the classic passage on the subject makes plain.

When thou art come into the land which the Lord thy God giveth thee, thou shalt not learn to do after the abominations of those nations.

There shall not be found among you any one that maketh his son or his daughter to pass through the fire, or that useth divination, or an observer of times, or an enchanter, or a witch,
Or a charmer, or a consulter with familiar spirits, or a wizard, or a necromancer.
For all that do these things are an abomination unto the Lord: and because of these abominations the Lord thy God doth drive them out from before thee. Deut. 18:9-10

God forbade His people to attempt to utilize the occult realm through infant sacrifice (abortion), to use any form of divination, to observe times (as in horoscopes, astrology), to use spells or enchantments (i.e., sorcery) and witchcraft, their services or spells (including charms and the use of drugs for spells) mediums, (those who consult with familiar, or "family" spirits) wizards (sorcerers, enchanters) and finally to be avoided are necromancers, (those who practice necromancy, i.e., contacting the dead as is done in channeling, by mediums, or spiritualists). All are to be avoided, and all are forbidden! God makes it clear that there is only one true route of access to Him, and to His wisdom.

Thou shalt not bow down thyself to them, nor serve them: for I the Lord thy God am a jealous God, visiting the iniquity of the fathers upon the children unto the third and fourth generation of them that hate me.

Exo. 20:5a

It is essential to follow the true route of access to God, for He here equates bowing down to, or seeking aid from, such false gods with *hating Him*!

Are you aware that demonic spirits can prevent childbirth?

DELIVERANCE FROM CHILDLESSNESS

During the first year this book was in print eight babies were conceived by women formerly diagnosed as "incapable of having children!"

This book offers the first real hope for certain childless couples...because, for some, there is a spiritual rather than a physical block preventing conception.

The testimonies included will build your faith as will the scriptural truths revealed. Surprisingly the Scripture says quite a bit about childlessness and gives:

* reports of at least nine unexpected or miraculous births granted to formerly childless or barren mothers;
* examples of women who were healed of barrenness;
* children granted in answer to prayer;
* instances of children denied because of *a curse of childlessness*

You will also learn:

* How curses of childlessness come into being, and how they may be broken.
* Ways that spirits of infertility and sterility enter, and how to cast them out.

Deliverance From Childlessness **$5.95**

Plus $1.50 shipping and handling.